Hull Then & Now 5

'It has been most truly said at our meetings that these old buildings do not belong to us only; that they have belonged to our forefathers, and they will belong to our descendants unless we play them false. They are not in any sense our property, to do as we like with. We are only trustees for those that come after us. So I say nothing but absolute necessity can excuse the destruction of these buildings; and I say further, that such a necessity has never yet existed in our time.'

William Morris, from an address to the 12th Annual Meeting of the Society for the Protection of Ancient Buildings. 1889

Kimberley Street 1904, looking east from Argyle Street
(Bill Longbones Collection)

Introduction

In all of the local history books that I have produced I have tried to emphasise the great importance of our architectural heritage – the old buildings that form the historic backbone of our city. There is a continuing trend (which started in the late 1800s) to sweep away buildings, which appear at first to have lost their function, and cannot easily be given new purpose. It saddens me to see that over a century later lessons haven't been learned, even in our more well-informed times. The outcry over lost buildings, still only seems to be heard once they are scheduled for demolition, or have already been lost. Whether that be officially demolished or mysteriously set alight over a weekend. I fully accept and appreciate good modern architecture, and we have many examples in Hull such as the Wilberforce Health Centre in Story Street, but we also have some awful 'new' buildings, which do nothing to enhance the street-scape or the buildings that surround them. In many cases the buildings that they replaced could have been adapted, albeit at a cost, to serve the same function whilst retaining the character of their neighbourhood.

Shops are something we all use, but the nature of them and how we use them, is in a period of great transition in the early 21st century. In chapter one I have shown a selection of shops from days past, in an effort to record how things were, and how they appear right now.

We all either have motor vehicles of some description, or use them on a daily basis. Their evolution from horse-drawn vehicles was begun in Hull Then & Now 4, and continues here in chapter two, with the transition to motorised vehicles. The convenience of the car is hard to balance with the congestion that the over-abundance of vehicles now brings, but the old vehicles shown here will hopefully remind you of more peaceful times on the streets of Hull.

The ill-advised trend to open-up all the older pubs that still had separate rooms, and create large open spaces, has backfired; pubs have lost their way. Large numbers continue to close, their large overheads leaving many of those that remain looking shabby and unkempt. The inability of the larger companies to understand that loud music, multiple TV screens, expensive yet tasteless beer, and all-day food is not what the majority of customers want any more, has caused a thriving micro-brewing revolution.

Smaller pubs need fewer staff and are more economical, and real ale – brewed locally has a taste that people will appreciate and pay for. An intimate and more peaceful environment will always turn heads. For these reasons, I believe it is the smaller traditional pubs that will survive in the long run. I'm not saying all old pubs were good – some were truly awful, and so was the beer, but the needs of the customer, the service and quality of produce they receive, is what will determine above all else, which survive and which don't. Chapter three is a picture of some of our pubs, past and present.

Please, enjoy Hull Then & Now 5, and I'll be back next year with something a little different.

Research, compilation, design, typesetting and publishing by me at www.paul-gibson.com

Printed and bound in England by Pureprint, Uckfield

ISBN 978-0-9568385-6-8

123 Hawthorn Avenue, 1905

Anlaby Road • 'High class fruiterer' John William Blanchard's shop was at 8 Anlaby Road, just near the entrance to South Street. Shown here c.1914 his was one of a short terrace of tiny shops that were squeezed onto a plot at the very beginning of Anlaby Road, which had originally been a stone mason's yard. Prior to his arrival c.1913, it had been a branch of photographer William Barry's business. The Blanchard family had several other shops in Hull, with a greengrocer's at 96 Cumberland Street, and a grocer's at 105 Perth Street recorded in the same year. John Blanchard left this shop in the early 1920s, and the terrace was re-fronted in 1935; it was later used by a wide variety of tradespeople including confectioners, stationers, carpet salesmen and hairdressers to name but a few. More recently the former shop has become a fast-food take-away outlet known as Gino's.

Anlaby Road, Regent's Terrace • Shown here in 1924 is property further west along Anlaby Road from Blanchard's fruit shop. The entrance shown on the right at this time gave access to Brook Street, which was redeveloped as Ferensway in 1930-31 (note the Theatre De Lux on the left of the junction). The notice in the window of Strelling Brothers notes: 'premises coming down', but despite their departure in that year the building was simply re-modelled, the top floor becoming a restaurant for the re-built theatre, which then became known as the Cecil. Following blitz damage during the Second World War the cinema, restaurant, and shops on the ground floor, were all demolished. The space left was partially used for the widening and extension of Ferensway in 1954 (the Cecil was re-located to a new building across the road in 1955). The gap remained mostly unbuilt however, until 1974-75 when the present Europa House was built and the corner set further back.

Hull History Centre

Anlaby Road • Directly opposite Strelling Brothers shop was this line of property, numbered 1, 3, 5 and 7, continuing beyond the Merchant Navy Hotel with numbers 13 and (just visible) 15. The photograph was taken as Ferensway was extended south beyond Anlaby Road in 1958. When the short extension was made a dual-carriageway in 1968, the first four shops shown here were demolished. Fortunately the former Merchant Navy Hotel (originally the Hull & East Riding Club) was spared; now known as the Gilson Hotel, it has a distinctive 1970s or 1980s extension that was built on stilts. The high number of Jewish tradesmen and shops in this area owes much to the transmigration of European Jews via Hull, mostly between 1891 and 1901. Many of the families remained in Hull, rather than continue their journey, and this accounts for the high number of tailors, jewellers, material dealers, etc, that once dominated the area around the station – many of whom became long-standing household names in Hull.

Anlaby Road • Further west, beyond the photograph shown opposite, was this interesting group of shops. Partially visible far-left of this c.1928 photograph was tailor Walter Abbott at 29, and at 31 The West Park Studio. The founder of the West Park Studio, Charles Pinchbeck, had moved his photography business here in 1919, opposite the Paragon Railway Station. Following the decline of photography as a hobby, and the postcard collecting craze, Pinchbeck diversified by selling the new fad of gramophones and records in the 1920s, but by 1936 the company was listed as a music dealer only. Next door was a pair of shops sharing one address; 33a had been the 'Anglers' Depot' of William Sydney Jubb, adjacent to Garside's Wireless Depot' at 33b. For many years now Garside's former shop has been home to Grannie's Parlour, where antiques and collectables can be found, and the former 'Paragon House' is currently being redeveloped.

Chris Hobson

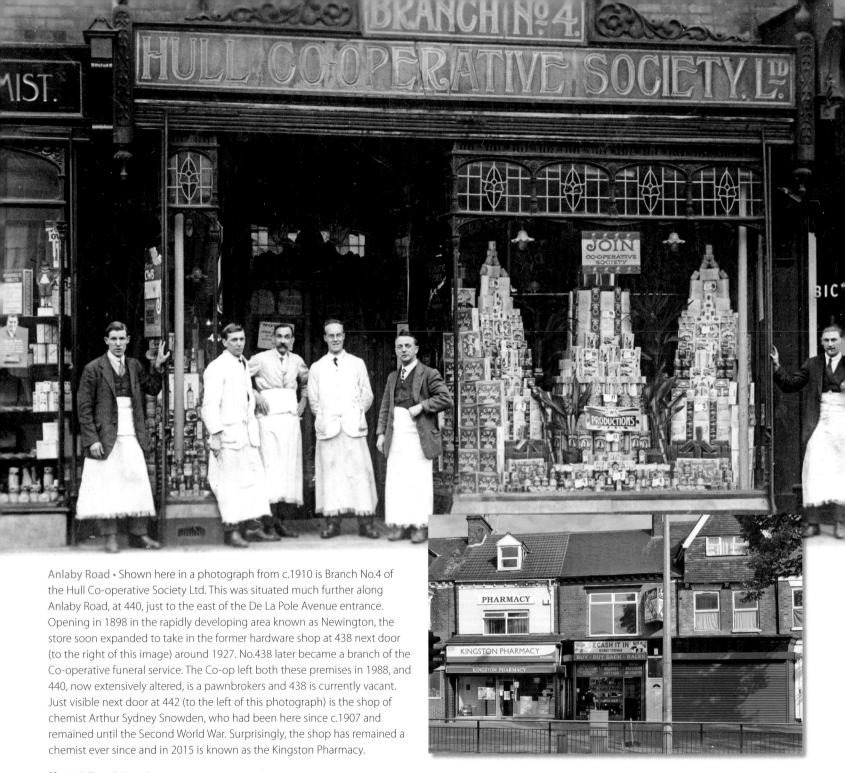

Anlaby Road • Shown here in a photograph from c.1910 is Branch No.4 of the Hull Co-operative Society Ltd. This was situated much further along Anlaby Road, at 440, just to the east of the De La Pole Avenue entrance. Opening in 1898 in the rapidly developing area known as Newington, the store soon expanded to take in the former hardware shop at 438 next door (to the right of this image) around 1927. No.438 later became a branch of the Co-operative funeral service. The Co-op left both these premises in 1988, and 440, now extensively altered, is a pawnbrokers and 438 is currently vacant. Just visible next door at 442 (to the left of this photograph) is the shop of chemist Arthur Sydney Snowden, who had been here since c.1907 and remained until the Second World War. Surprisingly, the shop has remained a chemist ever since and in 2015 is known as the Kingston Pharmacy.

Anlaby Road • At 489 Anlaby Road was plumber William Edwards' shop. Located just a few doors west of the Sandringham Street entrance, William's shop was one of a distinctive pair of purpose-built shops with accommodation above constructed c.1899. The Edwards were the first tenants of 489 and were first listed there in the trade directory of 1900. Shown here in a postcard photograph of c.1908, William was forward thinking enough to have a telephone installed and displays his national telephone number '11Y3' prominently over the shop frontage. The 1911 census records (John) William Edwards as a 45 year-old plumber & gas fitter, resident at 489 with his wife Frances Leah and their two sons George and Eric. The family remained here until 1914, and another plumber then took over the premises. Latterly a branch of Heron Frozen Foods, the pair of shops are now occupied by Carpet Kingdom who moved here from next door c.2013. The Edwards shop was the left of the pair, shown above in September 2015.

Beverley Road • This c.1911 photograph shows the short terrace of property between Vermont Street on the left, and the premises of the Hull & East Riding Institute for the Blind (HERIB) on the right. The properties were built c.1905, as seen here – three shops and two private houses adjoining.

From the left are grocer George Hutty at 478 Beverley Road, butcher John Thompson at 476, cycle dealer Donald Curtis at 474 and the private houses. Inevitably, the private houses were soon converted for retail use also.

Note the tram catenary pole in the older image, with ornate cast iron railings at the private houses. In the new image a tree is lost for a parking bay, and an ugly CCTV tower dominates the scene. In recent years the shops here have changed hands frequently, as they fall within an area with little footfall, awkward car parking, and a competitive supermarket almost directly opposite.

Beverley Road • Washington House, at the corner of Washington Street off Beverley Road, was built c.1890. It was part of the Washington Street development – consequently, when it was first listed in the trade directories it was noted as 'No.1 Washington Street and Beverley Road'. At that date, few properties existed further north along Beverley Road except for a handful of larger country houses.

The first tenant of Washington House was grocer and provision dealer John Williamson, who was recorded here from 1892. The terrace of four shops adjoining Washington House was built around 1895, and named Brentwood Villas – the stone name plaque remains. From 1898 Benjamin Smith Snowden was the tenant, and it is his name that can be seen on the premises in the photograph here, which dates from c.1910. By that time the shop was numbered as 432 Beverley Road. Despite Benjamin's death, the shop remained in the hands of his executors, his son Arthur Snowden continuing to supply groceries here until the late 1950s. Although it remained a grocer's for many years after the departure of the Snowden family, it has long been used as a Dove House Hospice charity shop.

Hull History Centre

Blanket Row • Francis and Elsie Hodgson had adjoining shops at 35 & 36 Blanket Row, just east of Finkle Street. The 18th century shop-front (shown left in the 1930s) hints at the property's age, although it was probably built much earlier, c.1600. The Hodgson family had been here since the 1840s, taking over an established bakery at the rear of the site, entered from the door on the far left of the picture, later acquiring the shop facing the street. The bakery closed in the early 1920s, but Elsie's shop remained until the 1960s. Little more can be said to emphasise the thoughtless destruction of this ancient street; Elsie's shop is shown below, just prior to demolition in 1978-80 with the rest of the block.

Blanket Row • In the same block, but at the opposite end of Blanket Row, was the shop of basket makers E H Potts & Co. Edwin H Potts took over 50 Blanket Row around 1904; it had latterly been a fish & chip shop for a short time, and prior to that a long-standing chemist's shop. The building had a very narrow escape in June 1915, during a Zeppelin bombing raid on Hull. The adjoining property on the corner of Blanket Row and Queen Street – the Golden Lion pub, was demolished soon after. The licensing authorities no doubt used the damage as good reason to end its licence, leaving the open land visible in both images. The photographs both date from c.1930; the lower on a Sunday or late evening as the shop is shut, and above looking east with the old Market Hall visible on the opposite side of Queen Street. Potts remained here until 1969, and from c.1950 also listed as a 'hardware and cleaning materials' supplier. Today, this view lies open across the cumbersome dual-carriageway that splits the Old Town in two.

Hull History Centre

Brook Street

Brook Street • Brook Street was one of several streets laid out in the 1780s, as the Infirmary was constructed in Prospect Street in 1784 (now the site of the Prospect Centre). Extending to the now foreshortened Mill Street, initially the street contained mostly private houses, as it was amongst still open fields. One house was for sale in the Hull Packet in October 1803:

> 'A Neat Modern-built DWELLING-HOUSE, situate in Brook-street, Hull; comprising a good Sitting-room, Kitchen, and Three Lodging rooms, with large Closets; a Pantry, and other Offices; a flagged Yard, and a Garden; and is altogether suitable for a retired family.'

In 1867 the street was extended to the railway station yard, which at that time stretched much further across what is now Ferensway, to the Paragon Street junction. As the town of Hull had expanded beyond the Old Town many of the streets around the town had become less residential and more commercial. In 1904 it was further extended to join with Anlaby Road. Shown here is a period of change, as the old met the new during the very early 1930s. Arthur Spreckley's old shop at 30 Brook Street was overshadowed by new offices and shops constructed during the ongoing development of Ferensway and the streets affected by its creation. A confectioner had long-occupied this shop prior to Spreckley arriving c.1921, when the premises were listed in the directories as 'grindery stores'.

Mr Spreckley continued to trade here until c.1930, despite the close-shave with the redevelopment shown in the c.1932 photograph top-left, when no.32 next door was demolished for the building of Brook Chambers. His shop finally closed following his death in 1933. The small door on the right led to Brook Court, one of many courts off the West side of the street, and became a goods entrance following the demolition of the houses and business premises within during the 1920s. Spreckley's shop was taken in when Bloom's extended (see opposite); the vacant shop-front shown above has been a Cooplands since c.1997.

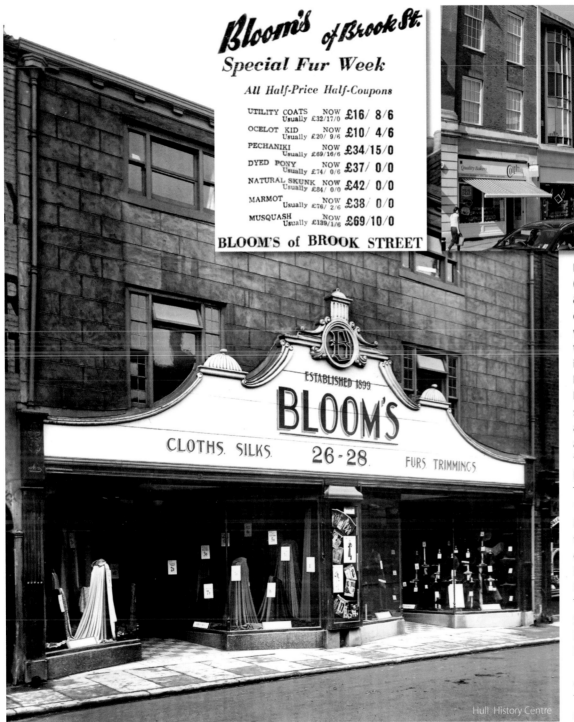

Bloom's *of Brook St.*

Special Fur Week

All Half-Price Half-Coupons

UTILITY COATS	NOW	£16/ 8/6
Usually £32/17/0		
OCELOT KID	NOW	£10/ 4/6
Usually £20/ 9/6		
PECHANIKI	NOW	£34/15/0
Usually £69/16/6		
DYED PONY	NOW	£37/ 0/0
Usually £74/ 0/6		
NATURAL SKUNK	NOW	£42/ 0/0
Usually £84/ 0/0		
MARMOT	NOW	£38/ 0/0
Usually £76/ 2/6		
MUSQUASH	NOW	£69/10/0
Usually £139/1/6		

BLOOM'S of BROOK STREET

ESTABLISHED 1899

BLOOM'S

CLOTHS. SILKS.　26-28.　FURS. TRIMMINGS

Hull History Centre

Brook Street • Nos.26 & 28 Brook Street (right to left) was the shop of Morris Bloom & Sons, silk & cloth merchants. Despite their claim on the signboard that the company was established in 1899, it was not until 1910 that Morris Bloom was first recorded in Hull, in the Kelly's trade directory of that year. He was noted as a simple cap maker, at 28 Brook Street – the left half of the property as seen here. The 1911 census lists him here as a 46 year-old with his wife and six children, all born in Lierpety, Russia; Morris noted 'Hebrew' in the nationality column of his hand-written census return.

The shop is shown here c.1936, and from 1937 (Morris died in 1937) Bloom's was listed as 26, 28 and 30 Brook Street, having taken in Spreckley's old shop and no.26 (see opposite). By the 1940s Bloom's were a well-known name in Hull, specialising in furs, as indicated in the 1949 advertisement above. The whole site was redeveloped after the Second World War following the extensive bomb damage to this area, particularly Prospect Street. The upper floors of Brook's 1950s store remain unchanged, but now divided into separate units at ground level. The company remained in Brook Street, and shop continued to trade until at least 1977.

Corporation Telephone:

1939.

TREVER & ENGLAND

BUCKLEYS

7 & 8. SCHOOL BOOK. KINDERGARTEN & STATIONERY STORES. 7 & 8.

OUR NEW PREMISES:

CARR LANE, HULL.

PRIMARK

Carr Lane • This promotional postcard was produced c.1908 by Trever & England, to advertise their 'new premises' at 7 & 8 Carr Lane. The company was first listed at Grosvenor Buildings, a stylish line of shops and offices further west along Carr Lane, which centred around the opulent Grosvenor Hotel that was built in 1891-92. Their shop (nos.1 & 2 Grosvenor Buildings) was next door to the hotel entrance, and they were first listed there c.1895; this was also the first mention of them in Hull. Their 'new premises' shown in this photograph formed part of an older terrace of property, initially known as Queen Anne Buildings – at the east end of Carr Lane, near the corner of Waterhouse Lane. It was to here that they moved c.1908. By 1913 the company was known under the name of Mr England only, Mr Trever having joined former competitor's A Brown & Son. Mr England continued to trade from Carr Lane until 1935. The site of 7 & 8 Carr Lane, on the south side of the road – opposite the City Hall, was long the site of Willis's, and later Willis Ludlow, their store rebuilt c.1970, and now occupied by Primark.

Cave Street • This shop had been a butcher's and/or a fishmonger's since it was built in the early 1880s.

Seen here in another complimentary postcard, issued as a Christmas greeting in 1906, are Charles and John Hudson. They stand proudly outside their newly opened premises at 18 Cave Street, situated on the north side of the street near the entrance to Crystal Avenue, and not far from the Beverley Road junction.

Their venture was short-lived however, and by 1910 John is gone, and only Charles appears to have remained a fishmonger, by then listed at his own shop at 228 Beverley Road. No doubt the more visible main road location provided extra passing trade, compared to the side street. 18 Cave Street meanwhile was next home to a furniture dealer and then a second-hand book dealer, who remained until the Second World War. Cave Street was cleared under compulsory purchase from 1975, finishing in 1983. Modern housing and gardens occupy the site.

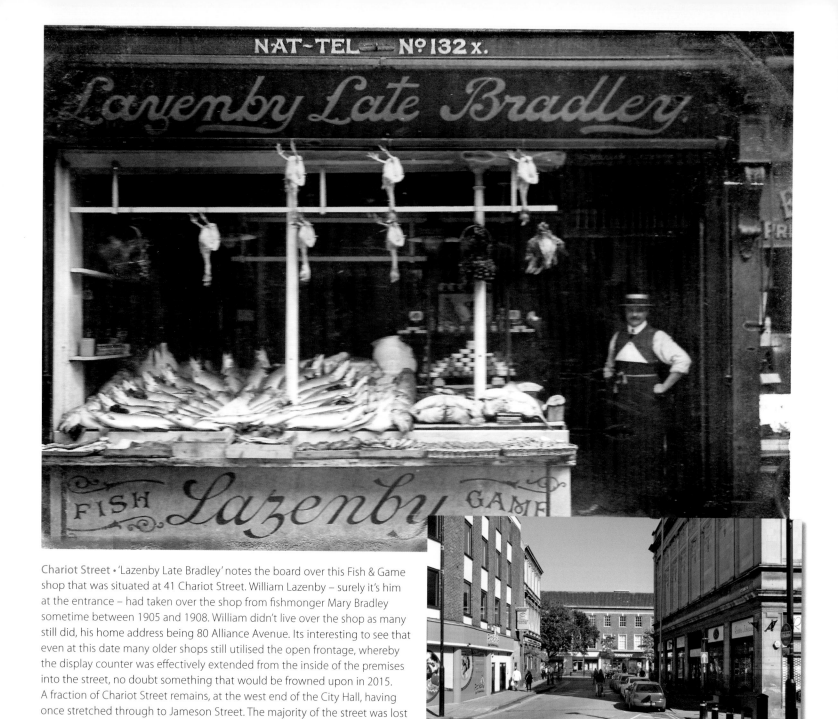

Chariot Street • 'Lazenby Late Bradley' notes the board over this Fish & Game shop that was situated at 41 Chariot Street. William Lazenby – surely it's him at the entrance – had taken over the shop from fishmonger Mary Bradley sometime between 1905 and 1908. William didn't live over the shop as many still did, his home address being 80 Alliance Avenue. Its interesting to see that even at this date many older shops still utilised the open frontage, whereby the display counter was effectively extended from the inside of the premises into the street, no doubt something that would be frowned upon in 2015. A fraction of Chariot Street remains, at the west end of the City Hall, having once stretched through to Jameson Street. The majority of the street was lost for the construction of the Queen's House complex in 1952; Lazenby's shop would sit somewhere within the inner car-park of the complex.

Charles Street • The good old Co-op, and several stores in one here, with butcher, baker, and grocer all under one roof. The staff here are stood on the sunny side of Charles Street (east) to pose for the photographer in one of a series of images that captured every branch at this date – c.1922. Initially just a grocery, in 1914 the Co-op took over 77 Charles Street, expanding to take in 78 next door by 1918. Following the departure of house furnishers Gibbs & Askwith, in 1922 the Co-op also acquired 79 Charles Street, and occupied the three bays on the far left of the block. 1922 was the date that the butchery department was added to the grocery here, suggesting a re-vamp of the frontage, and probably the reason for the photograph. The butchery closed in 1964, and the rest of the shop in 1968. The premises were re-used some years later thankfully, when the 'New Clarence' pub opened here, taking its name from the original, smaller yet much-loved Clarence, which stood opposite until its demolition in 1987.

Dagger Lane • Not in Hull – surely? Well, yes, I'm afraid to say it was. On the east side of Dagger Lane, a few doors from the entrance to Robinson Row, was this beautiful example of Artisan Mannerist brickwork (the stucco was added in the 1880s) dating back to the 17th century at least, probably c.1660. We can only speculate on its original use (see my web page regarding this building at www.paul-gibson.com) but it could have been an entrance into a larger property. In 1939 historian Tom Sheppard wrote that it 'dates back to 1570 ... originally the porter's lodge to an Elizabethan building behind it', but sadly gave no source for his information. As shown from the c.1835 drawing above, the frontage had remnants of a large doorway and a later, much smaller doorway. Despite its great historic interest to us in the present day, during the 19th century Hull was still fortunate to have many buildings of great age, and their value was not generally appreciated until too late. As shown from the Edwardian postcard (right), during the later 19th century a shop front was added; from the documentation available it appears to have been used as a shop (no.10 Dagger Lane) from c.1838 onwards. Despite it being given to the museums by the owner in 1931, using the excuse that it had become unstable due to nearby bomb-damage during the Second World War, the old house was demolished without protest in 1943, and nothing saved. Dagger Lane is a pleasant street in 2015, and the site of the lost building is marked roughly by the cream-coloured rendered house.

George Street • On the far-right of this image can be seen a fraction of the Grand Theatre, George Street, which gives an exact location for the shop of Oswald Fisher Walker. His window lettering states his business was established in 1870, but it was not until c.1892 that he was first noted in Hull in the trade directories as a 'hardware dealer' at 10 Lime Street. Oswald was only born in 1868, and it was his father Joel (a steel merchant) who had begun the business in their home town of Sheffield, Oswald arriving in Hull around 1890. From c.1903 his business was listed here, at 17 & 18 George Street, much more visible premises with a good passing trade. Oswald died in 1936 and the business ceased, although Frank Herbert & Co, tool makers, took over and continued trading until c.1941. The then re-numbered shop (29 & 31) passed to toolmakers T S Kaye from c.1942, following bomb damage to their old shop at the corner of Bond Street and Smeaton Street. The company remained here until its demolition in 1987, when the current buildings were constructed, latterly used as a bar.

Great Passage Street • Branch no.10 of the Co-op was opened in 1902, at 42 Great Passage Street – the corner of Fawcitt Street – visible on the right. The property had been a grocer's almost since it was built c.1790-1800. Note on the side window a notice stating that 'shipping' was supplied; this was not a reference to home deliveries, but that shipping orders would be taken from vessels in the town and western docks. The shop survived two world wars, and several waves of council demolition, closing in 1964, and was demolished in the final clearance of the area in 1966-67.

All that remains of Great Passage Street is a section of its original curving alignment, foreshortened by Ferensway, and now known as Amy Johnson Court after 1980s housing built on its north side and the site of the shop (the left of the modern photograph). Fawcitt Street was lost beneath the 1950s southern extension of Ferensway.

Great Thornton Street • 'Paperhanger' George Jewitt's shop was at 61 Great Thornton Street, shown here c.1904. He came from a long line of paperhangers in the Myton area, dating back to W C Jewitt & Sons, who were first listed c.1872 at 18 Hill Street. At that time there were around 26 paperhangers listed in Hull. By 1899 the following family members were also listed as paperhangers: Elizabeth Jewitt at 18 Hill Street, Hunsley Hewitt at 1 Strickland Street, Henry Jewitt in Porter Street, and William Jewitt at 159 Bean Street. George remained a paperhanger at 61 Great Thornton Street until the late 1930s, and the family remained (latterly as painters & decorators), retaining the W C Jewitt & Son name until c.1975. This shop was demolished in the 1960s, and the site is lost beneath 1980s redevelopment, which resulted in this section of Great Thornton Street being renamed Ice House Road. The shop would be on the left of this image.

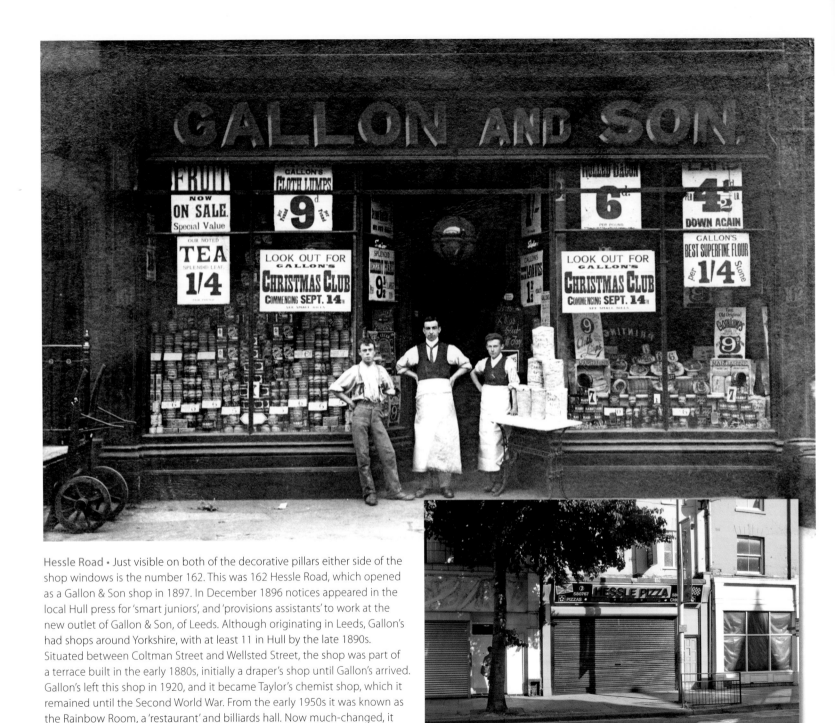

Hessle Road • Just visible on both of the decorative pillars either side of the shop windows is the number 162. This was 162 Hessle Road, which opened as a Gallon & Son shop in 1897. In December 1896 notices appeared in the local Hull press for 'smart juniors', and 'provisions assistants' to work at the new outlet of Gallon & Son, of Leeds. Although originating in Leeds, Gallon's had shops around Yorkshire, with at least 11 in Hull by the late 1890s. Situated between Coltman Street and Wellsted Street, the shop was part of a terrace built in the early 1880s, initially a draper's shop until Gallon's arrived. Gallon's left this shop in 1920, and it became Taylor's chemist shop, which it remained until the Second World War. From the early 1950s it was known as the Rainbow Room, a 'restaurant' and billiards hall. Now much-changed, it has been home to 'Hessle Pizza' for several years.

Hessle Road • Confectioner Sam Neal sold his shop at 230 Hessle Road in 1901. The sale notice in the Hull Daily Mail read:

'FOR SALE, Shop, good House, best position on the road, Mission Room and Aerated Water Manufactory at back, 383 square yards, good cart road; £1,600. — Apply S. E. Neal, 230 Hessle-road.'

From 1902 the papers regularly featured notices from W S Slingsby, who took over Mr Neal's shop. As well as furniture, Slingsby was also offering 'ready made suits for men, youths and boys from a shilling per week', and 'ladies capes and jackets, underclothing and baby linen' also from 'one shilling weekly'. William Seaton Slinsgby was an established furniture dealer, who took over his family's furniture business that was established in Junction Dock Street (Prince's Dock Street) in the 1830s. William later had shops at 116 Hessle Road and 5 Neptune Street, as well as showrooms in Tadman Street. Their new shop, three doors east of Constable Street, is shown here just after opening in an advertising postcard produced by Mr Slingsby. By 1910 this was their only remaining shop and by 1928 they had ceased trading.

W Boyes & Co took over c.1928, expanding their existing shops at 232 and 234, and now occupy almost the entire block.

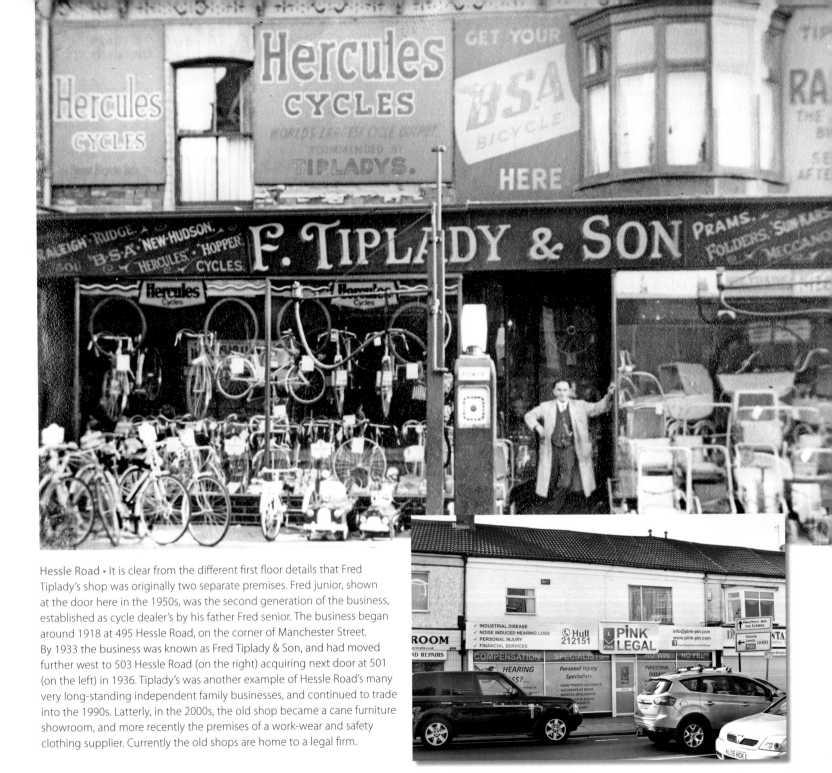

Hessle Road • It is clear from the different first floor details that Fred Tiplady's shop was originally two separate premises. Fred junior, shown at the door here in the 1950s, was the second generation of the business, established as cycle dealer's by his father Fred senior. The business began around 1918 at 495 Hessle Road, on the corner of Manchester Street. By 1933 the business was known as Fred Tiplady & Son, and had moved further west to 503 Hessle Road (on the right) acquiring next door at 501 (on the left) in 1936. Tiplady's was another example of Hessle Road's many very long-standing independent family businesses, and continued to trade into the 1990s. Latterly, in the 2000s, the old shop became a cane furniture showroom, and more recently the premises of a work-wear and safety clothing supplier. Currently the old shops are home to a legal firm.

Holderness Road • It may well be 36 year-old grocer John T Hance standing in the doorway of 145 Holderness Road, in this c.1912 photograph. Situated on the corner of Courtney Street, just beyond the old level-crossing heading out of town, this was a prime position on the busy shopping road, with heavy passing trade. The photograph was almost certainly taken when John took over this property in 1912, having just moved from his previous shop at 60 Wellington Lane, off Beverley Road. Lipton's had taken over the shop by the mid-1920s, following John's death. This section of Holderness Road was lost in the clearance of the area prior to the construction of Mount Pleasant in the late 1980s, leaving the site of Hance's Market under a grass verge. As I write, the area around the surviving Courtney Street is being redeveloped with more retail units.

Holderness Road • Further east along Holderness Road, at the corner of Durham Street, was one of the Lear family's butcher's shops at no.335. The Lear family business was begun in the 1870s, when John Lear was a cattle dealer in Beaumont Street, Drypool and Robert Lear a butcher in Witham. By 1897, the family business also included butcher's shops at 303 and 305 Holderness Road, and a farm in Preston; also listed in Preston was cattle dealer Valentine Lear. As Holderness Road developed, nos.303-305 were re-numbered as 330-335.

Two members of the family occupied the small adjoining shops initially, 305 being shown in this photograph from the 1920s. The family remained here until the Second World War, the last and longest resident of 333-335 being George E Lear, who is probably the chap shown here.

Today, the upstairs is easily recognisable from the patterns in the brick around the base of the window, but the ground floor is quite different. Latterly an estate agent's, the shop has very recently become an electrical appliance store.

Jennings Street • In 2015 Jennings Street would seem an unlikely place for 'the best and cheapest watch & clock repairing shop in Hull', but when this area was packed full of workers' housing – who all needed to get to work on time – it was almost essential. Seen outside his shop at 48 Jennings Street is Arthur Samuel Barber, around 1908 when he first traded from this address. Despite his appearance Arthur was barely 50 at the time of this photograph. The 1911 census reveals he was born in Suffolk and had been in Hull around eight years. His home address was a two-up, and two-down house at 12 Penzance Gardens off Cornwall Street, where he lived with his wife and six children. Arthur remained at this shop, on the south side of the street for just a few years, and by 1912 it was occupied by a general shopkeeper and no further trace of Arthur can be found in Hull. All of the shops and housing in Jennings Street were cleared by the late 1960s. Arthur's shop would have been on the left of the view below.

King Edward Street • King Edward Street was laid out in 1901 to create a more direct route from Monument Bridge and the Old Town, to Prospect Street. Previously travellers had to make a winding journey around the narrow 18th century streets, such as Waterworks Street, St John's Street, and Chariot Street. The British Gaslight Company had supplied gas to Hull since 1826, from their gasworks in Bankside, and had a large office in Baker Street. In 1905 the company opened this stylish showroom at 30 King Edward Street, near to the corner of Jameson Street; a contemporary newspaper report described it as:

> '... beautifully fitted-up and decorated in a scheme of white, crimson, green and gold (these being the colours of the embossed leather coverings of the walls). This is the work of Mr F Levitt of Beverley-road. On the second and third floors are large storerooms for all classes of fittings, and in the basement the heavier fittings are stored. The premises were a blaze of light, and yet a soft gentle grateful light. 'Incandescence' is the key-note of the scheme. As illustrated in the window of the 'shop', incandescent lights are to revolutionise domestic lighting.'

The gas company remained here until 1924, when the showroom was moved to larger premises at the corner of Prospect Street and Story Street, which remain to this day. Tailor's Goldstein & Co took over the King Edward Street shop at that time. What remained of this block of property after the heavy bomb damage in this area was demolished in the early 1950s for the construction of the present neo-Georgian buildings. In 2015 the site, now re-numbered, is marked by a careers guidance centre.

King Edward Street • Opposite the British Gas Light Company showroom, was Richard Field's 'The Octagon Cafe' and Noah's Ark toy department, at 25-27 King Edward Street. Richard was part of a family of tea dealers and grocers established at 11 Market Place by William Field in the 1830s. Field's cafes were such a success that they had spread to Bridlington, Leeds, Scarborough, Filey, Sheffield, Huddersfield and elsewhere by the First World War and employed 355 staff. Already famous for its elaborate shop at 54-55 Savile Street (see page 51), in the winter of 1902 Field's opened this latest venture on Hull's new shopping street.

Various musical acts were booked to play in the prestigious new cafe, with performances at 12:30 to 2:30, 3:30 to 5:00, and 7:30 until 9:30 daily. Shown in performance c.1904 in the lower photograph, is 'Miss Kate Erl's Orchestra of Ladies'. Miss Erl's ladies performed here for many years after the cafe's opening, noted as 'the only ladies orchestra ever permitted to play before the late Queen Victoria'. As well as this shop, and that in Savile Street, by the Second World War Richard Field & Son had shops in Beverley Road, Anlaby Road, Hallgate Cottingham, and Ferriby Road Hessle, as well as a bakery in Providence Row, a warehouse in Market Place, and their registered office in Dock Street. The 1939 trade directory lists them as 'grocers, provision merchants, cafe proprietors, confectioners, Italian warehousemen and chocolatiers'. This end of King Edward Street suffered badly during the Second World War blitz, and the cafe was heavily damaged in the same raid that caused the tragedy at the Prudential Buildings just yards away. The site was rebuilt as part of the Queen's House development of shops and offices in 1952, and the site of the Octagon Cafe is partly occupied by a travel agent.

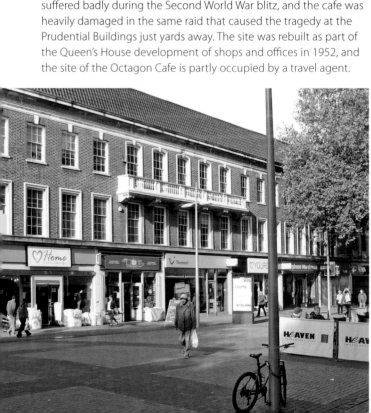

King Edward Street • Further north along King Edward Street, beyond the Jameson Street junction, was this pair of shops. On the far left is the entrance to Waltham Street, where the premises of photographer's Parrish & Berry can just be glimpsed, and on the corner 'merchant tailor' Thomas Arthur Glew's premises. Glew's had previously been at 5 Chariot Street, next to the Neptune Hotel, and the business moved to this address when newly-built in 1902. Soon after they moved to smaller premises in Prospect Street, but this shop remained a tailor's being home to Johnson The Tailor, and latterly Horne's in the 1950s. Florence Smith's millinery shop, visible next door on the right in this c.1905 photograph, taken over by the larger tailor's premises during a later expansion.

Since 1963 Alan Boyson's 'Three Ships' mural on the former Co-op building (long the home of British Home Sores) has dominated this corner. The concave concrete screen measures 64 feet by 66, and the artwork itself consists of 4,224 12-inch-square slabs, each made up of 225 Italian glass cubes. In total there are said to be 1,061,775 pieces.

Lowgate • 'Practical Cycle Maker' Henry Rodgers stands outside his shop at 7 Lowgate in this photograph; note the cycle wheel hanging from the large gas lamp on the left. Henry was born in Sheffield in 1856 or 1857, and was married with four daughters at the time of this photograph, which was probably made to commemorate the opening of his shop c.1910. Prior to 1910 the shop was empty for a year or two, but had previously been a tobacconist's for many years. This was also the Rodgers family home, and all of them lived over the shop in this humble building, which almost faced the Town Hall.

Henry and his family are not listed at the shop after 1925, and it remained empty again until 1928. It was then taken over by a laboratory furnisher that developed into the more well-known company of Northern Media. Latterly it was in use by The Northern Analysts Ltd, who remained there until the demolition of this side of Lowgate in the 1970s. The site is now occupied by a small building at the rear of the City Hotel, alongside a car park.

Wilberforce House • Hull Museums

Market Place • Thomas Bach bought the stock and premises of Mr George Allen in March 1861, as Mr Allen was 'retiring from the mourning business' according to an article in the Hull Packet newspaper. The premises were 53-54 Market Place – on the far-right of the photograph shown here. Thomas was 35 at the time, and the 1861 census records him as a 'mourning draper', living over the shop with his wife and six young staff. The shop was on the west side of Market Place, near to the passage-entrance to the Blue Bell pub. Bach expanded the premises shop-by-shop until c.1890, by which time the 'mourning warehouse' stretched from 51 through to 57, as shown in this early 20th century promotional card. In 1910 Thomas Bach & Co gave up the business, and all stock and premises were advertised for auction in the August of that year. The auction notice records that the private quarters upstairs included eleven bedrooms, three sitting rooms and a dining hall amongst many others. Nos.51 & 52 (far-left) were then used by a company called Gaiety Sports Ltd, as a 'sports saloon'. Following a shooting incident in the hall in June 1913 the company remodelled the property as a cinema hall known as the Gaiety Picture House, which was licensed in January 1914, but closed soon after, in March 1915. The cinema then became the Gaiety Theatre and later the Playgoers Theatre, which closed in 1934. The property suffered blitz damage in the Second World War, the plot remaining partly empty for many years. Around 1990 the majority of the site was used for the extension of the old Market Hall, creating what is now known as Trinity Market. Only the frontage of the re-modelled former theatre section of the block now remains from the original structure. Shown left is an original 1886 Bach & Co bill-head.

Bill Longbones

W. McLEOD UNDERTAKER

WILLIAM McLEOD
HARDWARE STORE

FUNERAL DIRECTOR
NAT TEL 163Y
FROM 4 ADELAIDE STREET

Midland Street • The McLeod family had been in business in the South Myton area since c.1830, when Benjamin was listed as a shopkeeper in Great Passage Street, and William a joiner in Adelaide Street. Around 1850 William added 'undertaker' to his trades of joiner, builder and ironmonger at 4 Adelaide Street. William McLeod's business had lately moved from 4 Adelaide Street to 17 Midland Street, prior to this c.1903 photograph, as noted on the right-hand window the new premises. William was joined by his brother Benjamin in the funeral business during the 1880s, both based at separate premises in Adelaide Street. The McLeods remained as undertakers in Midland Street until the late 1920s, the shop by then re-numbered as 14. Ideal Printers moved in to 12 Midland Street in the 1930s, and by the early 1960s had extended into the former undertaker's premises. Today it is used by a driving school, who have retained the 'Ideal' name.

Newbridge Road • The slow camera shutter-speed caused dairyman and confectioner Tom Smith to appear as a ghostly figure in this c.1904 image, which shows the shop front of his 'Reliance Dairy' at 147 Newbridge Road. Produced as a postcard by photographers Chadwick & Allen of nearby Rosmead Street, it was posted in December 1904. The street was still being developed at that time, and built-upon with houses and shops, the gap on the left soon being filled with another pair of houses of a slightly different design (note the different stones over the bedroom windows). In 1909 Tom relocated to 99 Newbridge Road, at the corner of Morrill Street, where in that September he was advertising for a 'Smart Lad with character, age from 15 or 16, to deliver milk Good wages to suitable...', and in 1921 for a 'Smart Girl, 18 or 19, for milk round...'. The business was for sale in July 1932, complete with 'dairy behind'. The original premises shown above have been converted for private use, no.145 adjoining having had a full new front and shorter new first-floor windows.

Newbridge Road • In June 1902 Joseph Winsall was advertising in the Hull Daily Mail for a '... steady man, must be a good bread hand'... , for his new 'Southcoates Bakery' at 44 Newbridge Road, at the corner of Belmont Street. His property, staff and vehicles are shown here c.1908. He had previously been at premises in Courtney Street, having been a baker in Hull since 1894. His skills as a baker won him many awards, including the Northern Counties championship and silver cup for Hovis bread in 1908. In 1912 he left Newbridge Road and opened his East Park Bakery at 530-32 Holderness Road. In 1915 he added an extra shop at 149 Holderness Road, and continued as a baker until the 1930s. His old bakery at Newbridge Road was then home to bakers Cotterill's and then Darke's, and in 1937 A.C. Skelton & Son took over, remaining until the early 1960s, by which time they had shops all around Hull and district, and the bakery had moved to Lorraine Street. Winsall's former bakery shop is now home to a unisex hair salon.

Newbridge Road • Just three doors from the junction with Rosmead Street, 88 Newbridge Road was still fairly new at the time of this c.1910 photograph. My guess is that it's William Mackman on the right of this sombre looking group, which shows the staff of his boot making and repairing shop. He was 20 at the time of the 1901 census, his brother Ernest 18, and Alfred 14. William was noted as a shoe maker and his brothers as apprentice shoe makers, all living in Lee Smith Street. By the 1911 census William, his new wife and a family of two sons and a daughter, are living here at 88 Newbridge Road. By 1913 the three elder Mackman brothers had their own boot repair shops around Hull, William remaining here until the Second World War when his shop and those of many of his neighbours were demolished following bomb damage. The site has remained empty since, leaving only 84 Newbridge Road standing alone at the corner of Rosmead Street.

Newbridge Road • It's rare to see such elaborate window displays these days, but a century ago it was commonplace. Before the internet and television, the shop front was the only way to promote your goods and services apart from expensive newspaper advertising. This particular shop was the Co-op's grocery branch no.19, on the corner of Dene Street – just visible on the left. It opened, newly-built, in 1908 and is shown here not long after opening. In 1929 the premises were expanded to take in a private house at 199 next door (on the right), as a butchery department; the butchery closed in 1964, whilst the grocery department lasted until 1967.

This west end of Newbridge Road has seen many changes since the 1960s, and there has been much rebuilding in recent years that has brought new life to the shopping area following a difficult few decades where these shops changed hands rapidly. Three entirely different trades now share the short terrace, hoping to do well from the upturn in the fortunes of the area.

E. PARKER, Pastrycook and Confectioner,
70, NEWLAND AVENUE, HULL.

Newland Avenue • In March 1903, a former confectionery business at 70 Newland Avenue was advertised 'for disposal' in the Hull Daily Mail. The new owner was pastry cook and confectioner Edward Parker, who took over the premises soon after. This promotional postcard no doubt shows his family at the door. The shop was the fourth property along from the corner of De Grey Street. His tenancy was short-lived here however, as by 1911 he was gone. The shop remained a confectioner's until the late 1930s when it became a stationer's complete with Post Office facilities.

The first four properties from the De Grey Street corner (64-70) were severely damaged by bombing during the Second World War. The site was rebuilt in the 1950s as a new showroom for house-furnisher's Teals, who remained until the early 1990s. When Teals left the premises became Newland Avenue's first pub, known as the Hogshead. Since then the pub has changed names several times, and is now Newland Tofts Lane Bar & Grill. Parker's shop would have been the section on the far-left.

Norfolk Street • This typical back-street corner shop was at 3 Norfolk Street, off Beverley Road. Situated at the corner of Russell Street it was ideally placed for all of the surrounding housing and several nearby pubs. It is shown here in a postcard from c.1910 when it was still being run by 75 year-old grocer Amelia Garbutt. Amelia had been here since c.1872, and the shop had been a grocer's for many years prior to her arrival. The 1911 census tells us that Ottringham-born Amelia was widowed and hence the head of the household. Also present were two of daughters – Elizabeth (45) and Edith (42), both single. Amelia died in 1914, at 3 Norfolk Street, and by 1915 Annie Elizabeth Garbutt was listed as a grocer here; Annie was the third daughter of deceased Amelia. The Garbutts remained until the late 1920s, following which several short-lived grocers held the property. Most of this area was cleared under Compulsory Purchase in 1939 (see Hull Then & Now 4 for full details) what remained being demolished in the 1950s. Today the site of the shop is a garden belonging to housing built in the early 2000s.

Paradise Row • 'As old as you like' ... my old friend Chris Ketchell would have said; in actual fact this corner shop was built as part of a block of three houses in the 1770s. Situated at the north end of Paradise Row (note the Georgian name plate) and the end of Little Mason Street, the three houses were built as private dwellings but soon mostly converted to shops, as were many in the street. The opposite side of the street was taken up by a large seed warehouse that was later replaced by St Philip's Church.

No.8, at the corner with the beautiful Georgian shop window, was a general shop almost all of its life, except for a short period in the 1830s when John Hunter ran a 'beer house' from the premises. This end of the street was demolished c.1914, and the site was later used as an extension of the Register Office that was only recently demolished, in July 2013.

The site is now used as a car park.

Paradise Place was re-named Carroll Place in 1950 to commemorate the rather tenuous link with Lewis Carroll, author of Alice in Wonderland, whose grandfather once lived nearby.

Paragon Street • No.61 Paragon Street had been the location of the Pavilion beer-house from c.1867 until its closure in July 1922. No.62 next door at the corner of Chapel Street had also been a pub (the Railway Inn) from 1850 until 1910. Former music teacher, Russian-born Jacob Friedenthall transferred his 'Paragon Music Stores' to 61 Paragon Street c.1924, from nearby Paragon Arcade where he had been since at least 1904; he also had a branch in Hepworth's Arcade. Previously he had sold sheet music from a stall in the market since the 1880s. The top photograph shows the shop newly-opened (the door on the right led to 'Beethoven Chambers' upstairs) and the one on the right c.1935, following the demolition of the former chapel next door. The Paragon Music Stores remained until 1971, latterly re-numbered as 58-60. In recent years the site was used by a building society that extended from the corner of Chapel Street to encompass the old shop, whose upper floors can still be seen.

Paragon Street • A theatre was first built on this site in 1846, by Stephen Kirkwood, and was known as 'The New Amphitheatre', soon re-named as the Royal Amphitheatre. Re-named again in 1847, the 'Royal Queen's Theatre' is shown top-right in a rare image from the 1860s. The building stretched from South Street, along the south side of Paragon Street, to a point near the present Paragon Arcade; a huge building, that was very profitable due to its capacity of 1,200. The east end of the theatre was demolished in 1867 (seen as the entrances to the Gallery, Pit, and Boxes in the older image top-right) to create space for the Imperial Hotel, now the site of the much-refurbished and altered Portland Hotel and Macy's Bar. During the 1867 demolitions a shop was also created, using up the easternmost section of the hotel building. The remaining section of the theatre itself – at the corner of South Street – was later renovated to become the famous Tivoli Theatre, which opened in 1912, and was demolished in 1957. Bottom-right is an image from 1941, showing Second World War bomb damage to the easternmost section; the decorated pilaster details of the former theatre being clearly visible in the devastated shop frontage, with the Imperial Hotel adjoining on the right. This was the shop of ironmonger Samuel P Wood, at 10 Paragon Street, first utilised as a shop in the early 1880s when it was home to engineer Richard Norfolk. Later in the 1880s Norfolk was joined by Samuel Wood to form the company Norfolk & Wood, agricultural engineers, which it remained until c.1890.

Hull History Centre

Agricultural & Electrical Engineer Samuel Wood remained here at 9 & 10 Paragon Street until 1953, latterly trading as S P Wood Ltd, wholesale ironmongers. His rebuilt single-storey shop can be seen in the c.1942 image top-right, which he traded from throughout the Second World War. The photograph bottom-right shows the shop closed and with auction posters in the windows following a tragic fire, caused by fireworks, in which a director of the company died and several others injured. In 1958 the site was rebuilt as Zimmerman's Cash Furnishing Stores, renumbered as 57 Paragon Street, using 'Wallspan' curtain walling with coloured glass panels to eliminate the need for painting. The distinctive building remains, and was a branch of the Santander bank until 2014, but is currently vacant (see opposite).

Hull History Centre

Hull History Centre

Perth Street West • We don't always have to look deep into the past to see the change on our streets, as shown here with a property that began as a private house in Perth Street West. Perth Street was constructed in 1907, and extended westwards across Chanterlands Avenue following the closure of the Polo Club that stood on the land west of Chanterlands Avenue in the late 19th century (see Hull Then & Now 3). At the corner was 108 Perth Street, built as a block of four adjoining properties. By 1908 it was the general shop of Charles Johnson, and by the late 1920s confectioner and grocer Mr Cattle had taken over the shop. His name 'Cattle's Cash Confectioner' can be seen in the 1920s image top-right, and the number 108 over the door. He remained until the 1940s, still listed as 108 Perth Street West. During the early 1950s something strange happens with the numbering and the shop is allocated the new address of 47 or 49 Chanterlands Avenue – still with Mr Cattle as the shopkeeper, who remained until the late 1950s. In the 1960s the shop became an off-licence, under the Hull Brewery banner of Anchor Wines, as shown in the image bottom-right. In 1969 it was listed in the Yellow Pages as 108 Perth Street West again, and remained as 'Wright's Wine Stores' until at least 1992, when it was still listed as 108 Perth Street West. The property has been the location for Marlborough Estate Agent for several years now, and is rather confusingly also referred to as 57 Chanterlands Avenue.

Prospect Street • The Bradford Stuff & Fent Warehouse was the culmination of a business first set up in 1870 by draper Thomas Dixon, which moved to Prospect Street c.1887, at 90, 91 and 92. These were earlier Victorian buildings however that were replaced by those shown here c.1903. Re-numbered as 88, 89, and 90, the store was part of a five-bay building, the Ancaster stone frontage being similar in detail to other Edwardian buildings further south along the street. In March 1914, a serious fire broke out in the store, which destroyed the ground floor all the way through to the rear entrance in Story Street. The shop was soon refurbished, opening in the June of the same year. The building lost some stone detail from the roof level, and some window casings had to be replaced following the fire, otherwise the upper floors are unchanged from the c.1910 photograph shown here. Mr Dixon's business remained here until 23 July 1929, when the shop re-opened as the London Drapery Stores, which remained until 1937 when Levy the Tailor took over. The shop remained in the clothing trade into the 1970s, but more recently (since c.2008) the shop has been a Hi-Fi store.

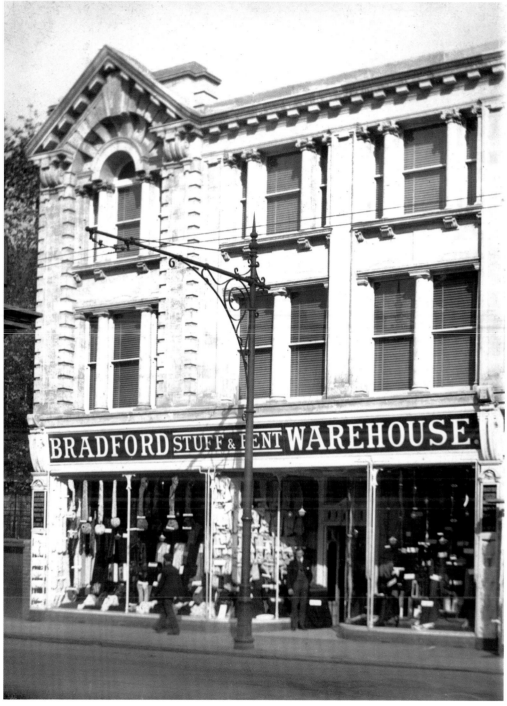

21, Queen St & Blackfriar Gate, Hull.

Queen Street • 21 Queen Street, at the corner of Blackfriargate (on the left), is shown here in a promotional postcard made for the occupants Cuthbert & Co around 1910. India rubber merchants, Cuthbert & Co had been here just a few years and were gone by 1912.

The location of the building was reflected in the trades of its occupants over the years, being in the busy road that led to the pier and ferry, and directly opposite the old Market Hall and Shambles on the opposite side of Blackfriargate. In 1811 it was advertised as an Ironmongery & Button Warehouse, opposite the 'New Shambles', and by 1819 was home to fruiterer Mrs Green, although these may have been in earlier buildings than this four-storey property. At the turn of the century a rapid succession of owners saw pawnbrokers, jewellers, clothiers, fancy goods dealers, cycle dealers, and even 'The City Curiosity Shop' inhabiting the shop in a period of little more than a decade. From c.1918 and up until the Second World War weighing scale manufacturers Avery & Co were probably the most long-standing occupants. Many properties in the immediate area suffered heavily in the blitz of 1941, and this corner property was also damaged and subsequently demolished. The corner site, opposite the entrance to Blanket Row, has remained empty ever since, and Blackfriargate is no longer accessible from Queen Street.

Savile Street • Built c.1790, the corner building shown on the right, at the junction of Savile Street and Dock Street, was home to many different trades and professions in the 19th century. In the 1870s for example, it was used by sculptor W. D. Keyworth, and at that time the rest of the terrace was also home to many photographers and other artists. William Field's origins are mentioned on page 33, but in 1890 his son Richard, also a grocer, took over Keywoth's premises at 54-55 Savile Street. The firm soon expanded to take in the entire block leading to Wilson's buildings and their 'Dram Shop'. Field's closed in 1973, and in 1976 these fine buildings were demolished for the present building, opened as Norwich Union House in that year. More recently the site of the former Oriental Cafe has been home to an army careers office and is currently a charity shop. The picture dates from c.1910.

Selby Street • This very distinctive, pointed, corner property was located at the corner of Selby Street, on the right, and one of Hull's lost streets – Parrott Street – on the left.

Ellen Auirila Wass is recorded in the 1911 Census as a 38-year-old licensed victualler, at 10 Selby Street with her husband Harry, son Harry, and one servant. The licence meant she could sell ale and porter, off the premises only, meaning this was what we call an off-licence. This was her first year at the shop, which still bears the sign writing celebrating the new king, crowned in 1910. It had long been a grocer's shop, which it remained under the Wass's tenancy, Ellen adding the attraction of ale, porter and tobacco to boost her trade. Just two years later the Wass family had left the shop following Ellen's untimely death in 1912. The licence was transferred to J H Dickinson in September that year. 10 Selby Street remained a grocer and off-licence until after the Second World War. The demolition of houses and whole streets in this area began in 1961; Parrott Street was completely lost, with clearance continuing into the late 1980s. The site of the shop is now an open grassed area north of the entrance to a 'new' street named Doncaster Street.

Short Street / Spencer Street • Grocer and beer retailer Joseph Stephenson can be seen at the door of his shop and off-licence at 76 Spencer Street in this 1920s photograph. Joseph and his wife Olive and their family had been at the shop since c.1918, and remained until its demolition. Clearance in this very run-down area, where most houses were classed as slums, began in the early 1900s, but it was c.1930 when the Stephenson's shop was demolished.

It and most of the other remaining property in the area was demolished for the construction of Ferensway, and a new Corporation Bus Station in Lombard Street. Situated at the corner of Short Street (on the left) and Spencer Street (right), the shop was just a short walk from St Stephen's Church, after which St Stephen's Shopping Centre is named. St Stephen's central arcade sits on top of the site of the shop, which is currently roughly marked by a Clarks shoe shop.

Spring Bank • It is most likely Friedrich Kress and Christian Wagner stood proudly outside their shop at 163 Spring Bank, just east of the former Tap & Spile pub. Pork butcher 'Fred' had began business at 45 Spyvee Street c.1899, but was at this address from c.1905 (prior to which it was a long-standing fruiterer's shop). Fred joined with another butcher Christian Wagner from c.1907, becoming Kress & Wagner and remained until c.1915 and the first Zeppelin raids on Hull. The First World War, especially after the raids, brought with it a huge distrust of even naturalised Germans. Despite this Fred and Christian's part in a deputation of naturalised Germans in Hull in May 1915, where they denounced the methods used by the German forces overseas at a meeting before the Lord Mayor at the Guildhall, the situation remained tense. The pair left Hull for the duration, Christian serving in the army as a cook from 1916. Despite this Kress & Wagner returned to business after the war, moving to another shop at 82 Welbeck Street by 1919, and returning to 163 Spring Bank in the early 1920s. Their company had several shops around Hull by the 1930s but the business later centred around the Spring Bank shop, where the family remained as pork butchers and bacon curers until c.1985. In recent years the shop has been used as a shop, but has very recently been converted for private accommodation.

St. George's Road • A rather poorly produced photograph, from c.1910, but with enough detail to convey that the owner had no doubt been at 237A St George's Road for some years. Situated on the east side of St George's Road, the shop had been built around 1884. Louth born Robert Freshney Howlett is listed at the property in the 1901 census as a 50-year-old grocer, with his wife Harriet and niece Alice Brocklehurst. Robert appears to have first arrived in Hull as mate on his father's boat the Edward & Hannah, where they were listed in the 1881 census, moored in Hull, his father apparently a widower at that time. His father, also Robert, set up as a grocer in Regent Street where they are both listed in the 1891 census. Robert senior died in 1903, Robert junior carrying on his business at St George's Road from c.1896 until his death in 1930. The shop, on the southern corner of Beecroft Street, was then used by a succession of grocers and butchers until its demolition c.1981. The whole of Beecroft Street was lost in the redevelopment of the area, and remains an open playing field. The name however, is remembered in Beecroft Court, on the opposite side of the road, nearer to the corner of Hessle Road.

Hull History Centre

Walton Street • 99 Walton Street didn't feature in the trade directories until c.1908, and previously numbers in the street had jumped from 93½ to 103, with none in-between. On the far left of this picture a clear break in the property can just be seen at roof level, suggesting this may have been an in-fill property built c.1906.

The first trade occupant was hairdresser Alfred Ernest King, who remained until 1920. In that year hardware dealer Walter James Leadley took over the small shop and house above. Born in Hull in 1870, Walter had five sons, the eldest being James Frederick, born in 1894; it is very likely to be James outside the shop with his father in this photograph. James took over the shop c.1926, probably the date for this photograph, and was first listed as a hardware dealer like his father. Entries in the directories soon recorded the shop as the 'West Park Home Requisites Store', and from c.1930 James was listed as a wireless dealer here, remaining at the shop until the 1950s. Walton Street was redeveloped in the late 1970s and early 1980s, when almost all of the original housing and shops were demolished, and today typically modest 1980s housing marks the spot.

Waterloo Street • Pawnbroker & Jeweller Philip Levinson was advertising for staff for his shop at 17 Waterloo Street in 1898, where he had been since c.1894. Philip was one of several sons of glazier Louis Levinson, all of whom were born in Poland, coming to Hull in the late 1870s. Shown right is the shop of Philip's brother, Lazarus Levinson, at 205 Waterloo Street and 91 Fountain Road, established in the early 1900s, which will be the date of the photograph; the brothers' shops ran concurrently for many years. Philip remained a pawnbroker, latterly as Levinson & Son, but Lazarus changed his business to that of a cycle dealer from 1925. Lazarus died in 1947 but the business was carried on by his son Victor as Fountain Cycles until 1972. It was then that this area was being demolished under a Compulsory Purchase Order.

The shop is shown bottom-right in the 1960s, and below in 2015, with old granite setts marking the point where Fountain Road crossed Waterloo Street.

Kevin Rymer

CORPORATION ELECTRICITY DEPT.

Show Rooms

CITY HALL BUILDINGS,

Waterworks Street,

HULL.

Waterworks Street • The Corporation Electricity Department was established in 1890, although a private company had been employed to supply certain streets in the town with electric lighting in 1880, but these were discontinued by 1884. The first 'information bureau and showroom' for the Corporation Electricity Department was the one shown here at 9 Waterworks Street. Opened in 1909, it was located in the shops beneath the newly-built City Hall; the interior of the shop is shown opposite. This showroom and shop remained in use until the early 1920s, when 'information' was made available at the original power station in Dagger Lane. As Ferensway was developed from 1929, a new 'Hull Electricity Service Centre' was opened there in large newly-built premises opened on 14 March 1933; the new offices and showrooms are shown opposite-below. These were demolished for the St Stephens complex, but the old Waterworks Street site remains in use, currently as one half of a school clothing shop.

Witham • 'Latest productions in footwear for 1913' note the advertising cards in each window at 20-21 Witham, a branch of Stead & Simpson Ltd. The heavily studded soles of the work boots in the doorway, and the various prices around the displays tell their own story. The shop was located at the busy junction of Clarence Street (just off to the left), Great Union Street and Witham, and had previously been a linen draper's prior to 'Stead, Simpson & Nephews' arriving in 1881. They remained here until 1937, and a variety of owners then held the shop, which was adjacent to the Holderness New Inn, which can just be glimpsed on the far right. From a gentlemen's outfitters and Jack's Gentlemen's Hairdresser in the 1950s, to a draper in the 1960s, the first floor retail area always had several individual companies letting the offices above. Latterly known as Munch Cafe, it is currently the Tidy Cafe.

Witham • On the opposite side of the Holderness New Inn was this hairdressing salon, at 23 Witham. It had been previously been a branch of the temperance chain of cocoa-houses, the Hull People's Public House Co. On the right in this late 1920s photograph is John Edward Adlard (known as Eddie) when he was working his apprenticeship at this shop (ladies downstairs, and men upstairs). The shop was damaged during the blitz of 1941 and Eddie acquired property in Holderness Road; this became well-known as Eddie's, with hairdressing at the rear and fancy goods in the gift shop facing the main road. No.23 Witham remained a hairstylist's, occasionally with a cafe upstairs, until the late 1960s when it became an 'off the record' club known as Movin' Scene. From 1975 it was known as Ocean 11, and the Paradise Club from the late 1980s (closed 1998-99). From 2001 it became Enigma, and I think Enigma was the first club to expand into the derelict pub building next door on the left. It is now well-established on the Witham circuit as the late-night Vega bar, alongside Jack Rabbit Slim's which opened c.2000.

Woodcock Street • Woodcock Street (originally Grafton Street) was laid out c.1874, with many streets intersecting including Saltburn Street – off to the left of this photograph. Fanny Maria Whelan was one of at least 17 grocers in Woodcock Street at the time of this c.1910 photograph. Her shop, at 216, on the corner of Saltburn Street, was not far from the Hawthorn Avenue end of this very long street. Lincolnshire-born Fanny was a 55 year-old widow at the time, and lived here alone. She had previously run an off-licence with her husband William in Short Street in the city centre; William died in 1905. Fanny remained here until her death in 1936, but the shop remained in use until the wholesale demolition of the area that began in the 1970s.

As shown in the present-day photograph, the site of 216 Woodcock Street is now taken by high quality, well-designed housing.

ACETYLENE
DEMONSTRATION VAN

"THE SUNS RIVAL"

ACETYLENE

THE
LEADING LIGHT SYNDICATE
LTD.
HULL.

Chapter Two

Motor Transport

ONE OF THE FIRST MOTOR CARS BUILT.

Mr Harold D. Smith, Works Manager of the new Hull City Garage, in the car. Taken in 1895.

The First Motor Vehicles • A Hull Daily Mail article in October 1896 noted:

'Everything points to a large "boom" in motor vehicles and there is likely to be a large demand for horseless vehicles from this district.'

Another article in the same month noted the appearance of the 'first motor car used by a tradesman in England', and probably the first motor car on the streets of Hull. This had been acquired by drapers Thornton Varley & Co of Prospect Street, and gathered a small crowd each time it stopped on its first trips around the city. Shown left is an 1895 illustration that was used in a Hull Daily Mail article of July 1906, describing 'one of the first motor cars built', owned by the manager of 'the new Hull City Garage' (see opposite). The advent of the first motor vehicles brought with it the arrival of a new phenomenon – the garage – a term that was first used from c.1900. In 1900 Mr Lavaggi, a cycle manufacturer of Grosvenor Street, was fined £1 for 'furiously driving his car at 10 m.p.h'. Mr Lavaggi's former cycle business had diversified to become the East Riding Cycle & Motor Co by 1903.

The Motor Act of 1903, which came into effect in January 1904, required every motor vehicle to carry a registration plate; clearly the lower the number the earlier the vehicle was registered. Shown above is a 1904 view of Beverley Road looking south towards the city from near the corner of Terry Street on the right. The car shown speeding along, but slow enough for the gaze of the passers-by to be caught by the camera, has no plate, and must date from pre-1904.

Motor Garages • At the Annual Cycle & Motor Show in 1900, held at the Assembly Rooms (now the New Theatre) in Hull, Hayter & Co advertised: 'all the latest motor cars'. Hayter & Co, originally cycle manufacturers of 24 Anlaby Road, had diversified to become 'Cycle & Motor Engineers'. In September 1901 they advertised for sale a:

'Second-hand Star Benz Motor Car, to carry four, Dunlop tyres, all spare parts, capacity for carrying oil for 200 miles, simple to handle, in perfect order ; two speeds, 6 and 16 miles an hour ; price £120.'

Specialist motor garages soon appeared in Hull. By February 1904 J C Walker had opened The City Garage in North Street. In July 1906 the Mayor opened another new garage at the south (city end) of Beverley Road owned by Hull City Garages Ltd, which:

'... filled a long-felt want amongst owners of cars in the city and district, and the popularity of the latest form of locomotion amongst a certain class.'

Shown above is motor engineer Ernest Wilson's garage in Wenlock Street, off the north side of Londesbrough Street, established c.1908. Next door, to the left, was his sibling's long-established cabinet makers' business; Wilson's garage remained here until the early 1930s. Parked outside are cars including an East Yorkshire registration BT-164, and LN-8270, which is a London North-West plate. The site has been rebuilt with council housing since the late 1970s.

Sculcoates Garage • Situated on the immediate right, as you enter Sculcoates Lane from Beverley Road, is a distinctive building that was once a garage and one of Hull's early motor garages, complete with a petrol stations. 2a Sculcoates Lane, was first listed as the premises of a motor engineer Sydney Davidson in 1915. By May 1916 it was known as Sculcoates Garage, run by Riseam & Co, Motor Engineers. William Riseam, motor engineer, is probably the chap shown in the shadows of these two photographs, which date from c.1920. The plate above the door reads 'private address 6 Cromer Street'; William's home was in nearby Cromer Street, just across the road in Sculcoates Lane. The garage was probably purpose-built c.1914, and remained in the hands of Riseam & Co until 1936; note the early petrol and oil pumps at the entrance, with swinging feed pipes above. From 1937 auto-electrician Stanley Surridge was based here, and remained until the 1970s.

Following many changes of use in recent years, the building has been a well-stocked antiques shop with furniture restoration services, since early 2015.

Petrol Stations • Large fuel 'filling stations', usually combined with a small supermarket-style shop, are fairly well-spread across Hull in 2015, and we also have the choice to buy from the filling stations attached to the huge supermarket complexes. Not too long ago however, much smaller, independently-run filling stations featured on our streets. The first filling station in England was allegedly opened in November 1919 in Aldermaston, but prior to that petrol was bought in cans from the chemist, and then the first motor garages; it was well into the 1920s before petrol filling stations became commonplace. The phrase 'Petrol Filling Station' didn't appear in our local trade directories or newspapers until the 1930s. In Hull, the first filling stations were at existing garages, such as those shown here and overleaf.

Below is the Regent Service Station, 241 Anlaby Road, just near to the Bean Street entrance - visible at the far-right of the smaller photograph. So called as it was close to Regent Street at the other end of the block, the garage was established c.1932 in premises that had been a butcher's for many years. In 1934, the Hull Daily Mail noted:

> 'Their stock includes tyres for all leading makes; batteries for all leading makes, including Austin, Ford, Jowett, Standard, Morris, Chrysler etc; brake linings; bulbs; and all leading makes of oils etc. They also carry large stocks of gaskets, bolts, cabon bushes, valves, pistons etc. If the motorist is in need of anything in these particular lines, he should try the Regent Service Station.'

Shown in photographs dating from the 1940s, the garage traded into the 1960s. The shops here were demolished for Rawlings Way c.1979-80, and the site of the garage is now modern flats.

Petrol Station • Top-left is a view of George Street from the 1930s. In the centre is scaffolding around the Queen's Hotel, now the Pozition nightclub. On the far left is the filling station and premises of automotive engineers and motor dealers Gray Bros & Kemp Ltd. This firm began life as the Embro Cycle & Motor Co in 1914, with works at the rear in what is still known as Charlotte Street Mews. The garage and filling station remained (latterly as Northwood Motors) until 1971, when the business moved to Hedon Road. The site of the former garage is now lost beneath the garden area of the new Trinity House Academy complex.

Bottom-left is the Carlton Motor Company, 468 Anlaby Road, complete with filling station. Situated just east of the old Carlton Cinema, this was a taxi office in 1921, becoming the North Road Garage & Engineering Co by 1926. Later taken over by Woodward, Young & Co, the right half of the premises was used as a sweet-shop by Mrs Young and later became Josie's Cafe, as seen in this 1950s photograph. The Carlton Motor Co was established here in 1951 and remained until the late 1970s. The company then moved to the 'new' Sutton Fields Estate, remaining until c.2005. The site of the former motor premises, filling station and Josie's Cafe is now occupied by Brownie's Bar.

Coach Builders • The new motor vehicles usually came in the form of a basic chassis and engine, and were fitted with bodies by local companies. Many old Hull coach-building firms accommodated this new business, transferring their skills honed on horse-drawn vehicles to the new horse-less variety. Edward Annison was a memorable early example, the Annison family expanding into all aspects of the motor trade from its inception. Examples of their work can be seen on previous pages.

Another, less well-known but equally long-standing example, was T. D. & W. Dales, illustrated in the advertisement opposite that dates from c.1910.

The firm was begun in 1837, and by the early 1840s Edward Dales was a coach-builder based in Great Union Street. Later moving to Ropery Street, they were advertising particularly as 'waggonette builders' in the 1890s, adding 'lurry', waggon and van builders by the turn of the century. The company continued to trade as vehicle builders until 1942, when a serious fire did 'considerable damage' to their premises, and they were no longer listed.

Coach Builders • Benjamin Barnaby came to Hull in 1871 and by 1872 was working as a blacksmith and later a wheelwright at premises in Hessle Road, re-locating to Neptune Street by the early 1880s.

Later known as B. Barnaby & Son from c.1920, and B. Barnaby & Sons, when the business was managed by sons George and John William Barnaby, following their father's retirement in 1923 (he died in 1936). It was from this date that they became known solely as motor body builders. As the number of motor buses increased, Barnaby & Sons specialised in this area and expanded from the normal charabanc and motor car bodies, during the 1930s, and began building single-deck buses and coaches, and less-frequently double-deckers. One of their stylish decorated invoices is shown left.

Becoming Barnaby's Motor Bodies (Hull) Ltd from 1937, the company was sold in 1960 and finally wound-up in 1974. Some of the vehicles it built are mentioned in the following pages. In 2015 our new vehicles tend to come ready-built, but specialist body paint and repair shops still exist.

Laundry Van • The sign-writing on the body of this vehicle records that it was built by former cab proprietor turned motor engineer Edward S Annison. He was a member of the famous Annison family of Hull, whose business had diversified over the years from their origins in the coach-building trade, ending famously as funeral directors from the still extant Witham buildings. The Commer van shown here (finished in bright red and brown) was first registered to Taylor's in 1913. At that time Taylor's Laundry (first established in Dock Street in 1863) were probably also still using horse-drawn vehicles to carry laundry to and from the premises. As motorised vehicles became readily available from the early 1900s, many added motor vans to the fleet, whilst retaining the cheaper horse power. Taylor's vans, promoted in the 1933 advertisement right, could be seen on the streets of Hull well into the 1960s.

TAYLOR'S LAUNDRY, Ltd.
UNRIVALLED
SPRING CLEANING SERVICES.
CARPETS, CURTAINS & COVERS
OF ALL KINDS, AND EVERYTHING FOR
THE RENOVATION OF THE HOME.
VAN SERVICE THROUGHOUT THE CITY, THE SUBURBS, AND THE RIDING,
INCLUDING BRIDLINGTON.
SOUTHCOATES LANE, HULL
Telephone 31896.

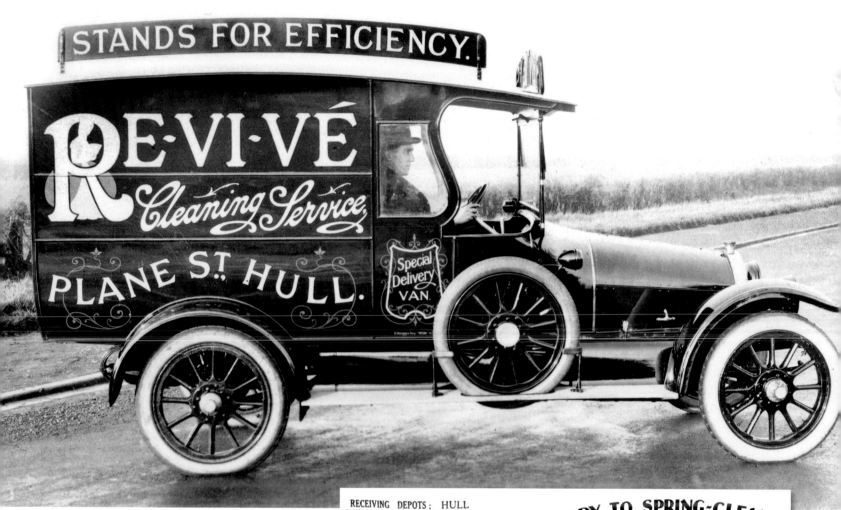

Laundry Van • Once again, the coach builder of this 1920s vehicle left their details on the bodywork; Barnaby & Sons, who were originally based in Neptune Street (see page 69). The Re-Vi-Ve Cleaning and Dyeworks was created in the early 1,920s as part of the Bentleys Snowflake Laundry, and was initially based at their works in Plane Street. Such was its success that separate facilities were built in North Road in 1928; the illustration shown right appeared in a newspaper article celebrating 25 years of Bentleys Laundry in 1928. Bentleys Snowflake Laundry became Bentleys Industrial Services in 1979, and survived until 2005 (latterly in Harrow Street) when the company closed.

RECEIVING DEPOTS : HULL

PLANE STREET.	64. JAMESON STREET.
NORTH ROAD.	75, NEW BRIDGE ROAD.
398, ST. GEORGE'S-ROAD.	2, TRINITY STREET.
248, BEAN STREET.	733, HESSLE ROAD.
390, HESSLE ROAD.	

THE NEW RE-VI-VE CLEANING AND DYEWORKS.

RE-VI-VE CLEANING & DYE WORKS

READY TO SPRING-CLEAN ?

Our RE-VI-VE CLEANING and DYEING SERVICE can save you money, and spare you work.

Covers, Curtains, and Carpets scientifically CLEANED or DYED to suit your favourite colour scheme.

Our COMPLETE CARPET SERVICE covers beating, cleaning, refitting, laying, alterations and repairs by our own Staff.

Have Dresses, Coats and Suits cleaned and made smart for Spring. The RE-VI-VE SERVICE will clean or dye them at a fraction of the cost of new garments. Mourning orders in 24 hours. Fashionable pleating in various styles. FREE Collection and Delivery by our Vans, within 20 miles of Hull.

MEN'S SUITS Dry-Cleaned - 5/6

RE-VI-VE CLEANING & DYEWORKS
North Road - HULL

Telephone : 32245.

HEAD OFFICE : PLANE STREET, HULL   Telephones : 2620 — 2621.

Delivery Truck • Thomas Hicks was originally based at 3 Brunswick Avenue, off Beverley Road, just a few doors from the surviving Brunswick Avenue Board School. His shop is just visible on the left of the 1904 image above, which looks west along the avenue towards Beverley Road, with the school on the left. He was listed there as a plumber from c.1903 until 1911, when the census of that year reveals Thomas to have been 38 years old, and Hull born. With him in the four-room house was his wife Laura (39) and their children Ethel (11), William (9), and Harry (7), all also born in Hull. In 1912 he moved to a larger property at 19 Brunswick Avenue, further west nearer to the Blundell Street entrance. The photograph shown centre-right was almost certainly taken around 1912 when he moved there. Note that the sign-writing states he was a plumber, electrician and contractor at that time. The photograph top-right was taken some years later, as by that time his signage notes T Hicks & Sons, indicating his sons were both of an age to work, which suggests a date of around 1920. His business was clearly doing well, and Thomas proudly displayed his delivery truck outside the shop at no.19, with its arched entrance to works and storage at the rear. The company of T Hicks & Sons remained in business here until 1968. The housing in this area, including both of the Hicks' addresses, was demolished from 1970 onwards, although some houses remain in Blundell Street to give a small reminder.

Chemist Van • Some old Hull companies remain in the memory decades after they ceased to be, and one of those is Owbridge's. W T Owbridge's cough mixture was a staple in most homes. Shown here are gleaming new vehicles from the company fleet; three parked in the yard behind the premises in Osborne Street (bottom-right) and another parked in an unknown location (top-right). Walter Owbridge began business in Hull c.1870 when he was listed as a chemist at 76 Porter Street in the Hull Packet newspaper, selling Banks' Cough Elixir as an official agent; in 1876 he began selling his own 'lung tonic'.

In January 1896 new premises were built in Osborne Street, using the name 'The Laboratory', as he had at his previous site in Porter Street. Designed by Hull architect T Beecroft Atkinson, the new buildings cost almost £6,000 and featured a landmark clock in its impressive central tower. The company was sold in 1969 and finally closed in 1972, but the 'laboratory' frontage remains. The enlarged site was converted to 35 flats in 1990.

Grocer's Vans • William Cussons delivery fleet included a variety of makes of vehicle, including Ford and International, several of which are on display above outside the Blundell Street Board School around 1920. As early as 1912 they were acquiring vehicles from motor-engineer E S Annison of Witham – an Hull Daily Mail article in October that year noted they had purchased the first motor-van in the city provided by the Commercial Car Co of Luton. Shown opposite is another motor-van, a 30 cwt model constructed by the company Karrier, in Cussons' usual green colour, first registered in 1923. The Karrier company was founded in 1904 as Clayton & Company in Huddersfield. In 1908, they started making Karrier cars and in 1920 changed the company name to Karrier Motors Ltd. The firm later produced buses and trolleybuses, most notably the Karrier 'W' model.

Cussons had garage facilities for their fleet in nearby Norfolk Street, behind their main shop and office premises that faced Beverley Road. The scene outside the now derelict, neglected school is a ghostly and sad one in 2015.

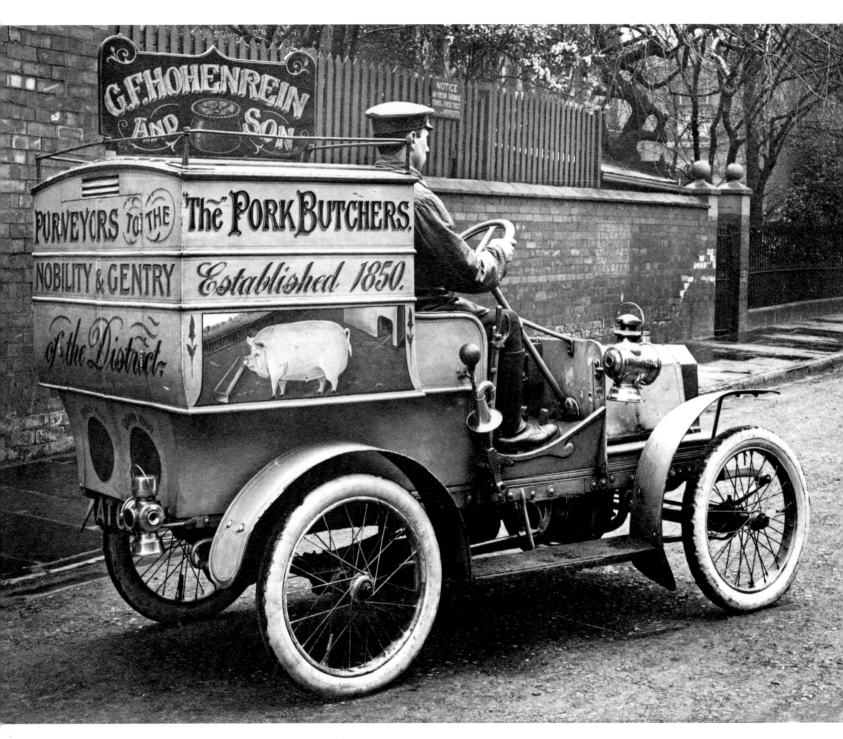

G.F. HOHENREIN AND SON

PURVEYORS TO THE 'The PORK BUTCHERS,
NOBILITY & GENTRY Established 1850.
of the District

Butcher's Van & Private Vehicle • Pork butcher George Frederick Hohenrein was born in Morsbach, Germany in 1832 and opened his first shop in Hull in 1850. It was in Hull's bustling Waterworks Street, at no.7, as shown in the c.1909 photograph on the right. He lived at Derringham Cottage off Derringham Street, and his household included five sons and a daughter. Son Charles Henry Hohenrein (born 1883), took over the business and is shown above c.1910, at the wheel of a smart new motor outside Derringham Cottage. Shown opposite is one of the family's beautifully coach-painted delivery vans at the same date, also parked outside the family home. After the Zeppelin attacks in Hull, at the start of the First World War, the family changed their surname to Ross in July 1915. Their shops in Waterworks Street and Prince's Avenue remained in use until the 1950s. In 1946 Charles retired to The Paddocks, Burton Pidsea, and later to his daughter's house in Cottingham in 1956. He died in 1974 aged 91.

Sweet Vehicles • Fred Needler first set-up his confectionery business in Anne Street in 1886, with a single horse and cart, but the vehicles shown here and overleaf date from the 1920s and 1930s when the company was at its peak and had over 40 vans.

Working from the purpose-built factory off Sculcoates Lane that opened in 1906 (demolished in 2003), the company mostly used Thorneycroft or Maudsley vehicles, coach-built by Barnaby's of Hull, and always in the trade-mark chocolate brown. The fleet was maintained until c.1965 when goods were increasingly transported around the country by rail and then in 40-foot containers to independent distribution depots.

The vehicles were also used for recreation, as shown opposite, where staff appear in fancy dress costume alongside a float created on a delivery truck for Empire Day. The vehicle was being displayed on Corporation Field in Park Street before parading around the city.

Needler's Vehicle • Seen here at the entrance to the Needler's Bournemouth Street factory in July 1929, is one of their trucks laden with chocolates and confectionery destined for New Zealand. It is surprising to note that a small local factory was supplying goods to such far off lands, but in the same month a report in the Hull Daily Mail noted that another load was destined for Bogota, the capital of the Columbian Republic, and that the journey would take the goods thousands of feet above sea level from the port of Barranquilla, along the River Magdalena, some 600 miles into the mountains.

Heavy Goods Vehicle • This was no.10 in Leopold Walford's fleet, and is shown here delivering to Alexandra Dock c.1921. Walford's opened a branch in Hull in 1919, and set up a new 'steamer service' between Boulogne and Hull in 1920. Further services were soon arranged all over the world from New Zealand to South America. Walford's remained in Hull until only 1923.
The waggon was one of the Sentinel Waggon Works' first steam 'waggons'. The company began producing these vehicles in 1915, and continued under several name changes until 1956 when Rolls Royce took over their works for diesel locomotive engine production. The Sentinel Manufacturing Co continues to trade from their Shrewsbury works.
In 2015 vehicles moving cargo in and out of Hull's docks are on a much larger scale, with most mixed cargo utilising Hull's state-of-the-art container terminal.

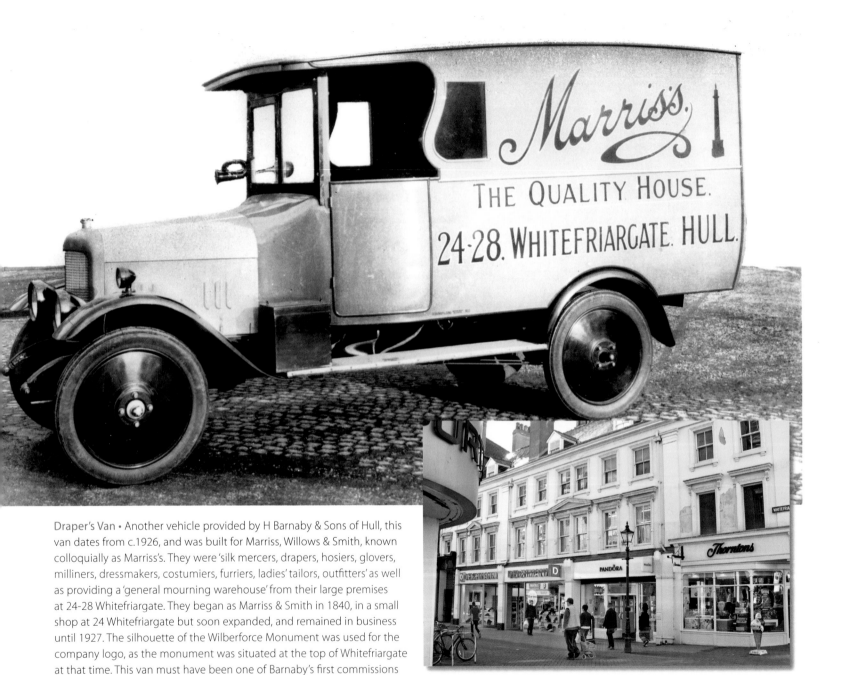

Draper's Van • Another vehicle provided by H Barnaby & Sons of Hull, this van dates from c.1926, and was built for Marriss, Willows & Smith, known colloquially as Marriss's. They were 'silk mercers, drapers, hosiers, glovers, milliners, dressmakers, costumiers, furriers, ladies' tailors, outfitters' as well as providing a 'general mourning warehouse' from their large premises at 24-28 Whitefriargate. They began as Marriss & Smith in 1840, in a small shop at 24 Whitefriargate but soon expanded, and remained in business until 1927. The silhouette of the Wilberforce Monument was used for the company logo, as the monument was situated at the top of Whitefriargate at that time. This van must have been one of Barnaby's first commissions as they only began trading in 1926; note the old style of car horn and distinctive spoke-free solid wheels.

The firm's imposing store still exists on the south side of Whitefriargate, although re-numbered, and now occupied by a shoe shop and a jewellers.

Platform Truck • W D Mark & Sons Ltd were 'hide and skin brokers' with depots around the country, but mostly in the north. They were established in the early 1880s, but came to Hull around 1914 and were based at 18 Sewer Lane, where they remained until the 1940s.

The side of their truck notes some of their other branches at Newcastle, Carlisle, York and other places, and they had branches in Scotland by the 1920s. The company was still trading around the north-east until the late 1990s. Sewer Lane was a sensible location for a hide and skin merchant as it was in this part of Hull's Old Town that many slaughterhouses were based. In 1899 there were five 'carcase butchers' in Sewer Lane along with three more in Blanket Row, and another in Robinson Row. Four hide and skin

merchants were also based in the Old Town at that time. At the time of this photograph, c.1925, Sewer Lane still had three 'wholesale butchers', with five more in the adjacent streets.

The Albion truck shown here was made by the Albion Motor Car Company, established in 1899, and known as Albion Motors from 1930. Initially the company only produced motor cars, but from 1909 it concentrated on commercial vehicles such as this. During the First World War large numbers of similar three ton trucks were ordered by the War Office, and after the war many were converted as charabancs. The company was taken over by Leyland Motors in 1951.

Blow's Steamers Lorry • David A Blow was originally a corn and cake merchant, based in his hometown of Grimsby. He is listed there, as a 37-year-old, in the 1891 census with his wife and family. By the mid-1890s he is recorded as a sloop owner in Hull, sailing from Oberon Wharf, at the rear of the old Oberon pub in Queen Street. By 1900, as Blow's Steamers, they were operating a regular service to Grimsby and David's son Nelson Blow took over in the early 1900s. In 1905 he was listed as a corn merchant, wharfinger, warehouseman, steamship owner and sloop owner.

Blow's Steamers survived until c.1970. Oberon Wharf, and its arched entrance that is visible in the 1940s image on the left, still exists in 2015 as a car park for firms based in the old pub. The tiny wharf can be seen on the far-left of the 1930s image above, where a line of staff look out across the harbour. Blow's new lorry shown above was produced by AEC (the Associated Equipment Company), who had their origins in a company established in 1855. They produced some of the first mass-produced commercial vehicles, and began large-scale production of this three-ton Y-type lorry in 1916.

William Jackson & Son Van • Shown here in 1908 is one of the very first vehicles bought by Jackson's, outside their Clarendon Street garages. It was a 19 cwt Humber van (cwt was the abbreviation of a hundredweight – 112 pounds – equivalent to 50.8 kilogrammes). Despite having a small fleet of vans and waggons by the time, it was not until 1931 that the company had their own garage facilities in Blundell Street; they had previously been garaged at the Victoria Street site. Several locations were then rented including that shown here in Clarendon Street. Thirteen of the company's vehicles were commandeered in 1939 during the Second World War causing Jackson's to return to horse and cart, buying 25 in the same year. Shortly after they also bought four steam lorries, as a precautionary measure against the threat of petroleum rationing.

East Hull Gas Company Steam Waggon • The 'Super Sentinel' Steam Waggon was first made available in 1923, following the creation of the Sentinel Waggon Works at Shrewsbury in 1920 (they had been there since 1915, see page 81). The company had its origins in Glasgow, as Alley & MacLellan, at the Sentinel Works, Jessie Street, Glasgow where the company was formed c.1875. This photograph of c.1925 shows a brand new Super Sentinel in the full livery of the East Hull Gas Company.

The Sutton, Southcoates & Drypool Gas Company was formed in 1846, from an enterprise begun by 'gas maker' John Malam in 1845; the Hull Packet newspaper ran a notice from the Sutton, Southcoates & Drypool Gas Co in April 1846, asking contractors to tender for the construction of the works in Sitwell Street. On 1 January 1907, its name was changed to the East Hull Gas Company, and in 1948 it was taken over by the North Eastern Gas Board. The Victorian gasholders at the rear of the Sitwell Street gas works, facing St Mark's Street, were demolished in 2013.

Hull Corporation Highways Department Steam Waggon • The vehicle shown here is one of the earliest steam waggons produced by the Sentinel Steam Waggon Company, probably a 'Standard' Steam Waggon, produced by the company from c.1906, and seen here c.1910.

In 1910 the Corporation decided to employ steam waggons for the clearing of snow, and in 1915 it was noted in the Hull Daily Mail that the Hull Corporation Works Committee had bought a six-ton Sentinel steam waggon for £550, but this was more likely to have been the model shown opposite.

Not everyone was pleased with the heavy steam vehicles on Hull's roads however, as in February 1912 a letter to the Mail noted that:

> 'Victoria-avenue, Park-avenue, Richmond-street, and Ella-street are in disgraceful condition owing to a steam waggon constantly passing up and down with heavy loads, ruining the roads of these fine Avenues, the admiration of everyone in summer ...'

Fortunately, steam powered waggons were soon superseded by petrol fuelled vehicles as more powerful engines were made available.

Removals Lorry • James Hardaker, born in Horsforth, Leeds in 1837, was living in Hull by 1869. The census of 1871 records him at his home in Prospect Street with his family of three sons and a daughter, his wife and a housemaid. By 1872 he was recorded as a general dealer at 17 Wellington Street, and was still recorded as a rully-man and general carrier in 1880. By 1881 the family had expanded to five sons and two daughters. From 1882 he was first listed as a removals man, Joseph Hardaker carrying on the Wellington Street carrier business. In 1891 he was offering 'town removals at two shillings per hour', from his 'spacious dry storeroom' in Wright Street. James died in 1918, though the business had been run by son Thomas since 1908, later passing to son John by 1914. The company was based in Boulevard from c.1905, but moved to West Dock Avenue following its sale in 1999, when the company ceased to be family-run, though it continues to trade in 2015. In 1926, AEC and Daimler formed the Associated Daimler Company, which dissolved just two years later; this Hardaker's maroon coloured AEC removals van was first registered in October 1929.

Milk Lorry • Parked on the old Corporation Field in Park Street, this decorated lorry was almost certainly awaiting a parade. Modern Dairies 'Clean & Safe' milk is proudly stated on their delivery lorry no.5, and the purpose of the display was to promote the firm as *the* supplier of 'pure homogonized' milk (a process that prevents the milk separating and forming a layer of cream at the top of the bottle). Based at 124 Lambert Street, and formed as a partnership in 1925, the company was dissolved on 15 November 1926, only to reopen again in 1927 as a solo enterprise. In 1931 the company was often in the newspapers, when a competitor was charged with stealing their empty bottles and filling them as their own. Later the same year there was controversy in the city when some dairies were found to be selling imported milk as 'local'. Modern Dairies soon placed an advert in the Mail clearly stating all of their milk was sourced only from East Riding farms, and claimed to be *the* pioneers of sterilized bottled milk in Hull. This gives a probable date for the photograph here, where they proclaim to be 'the pioneers'. Modern Dairies lasted until the 1940s, latterly from premises in Ryde Avenue.

Fish Delivery • This image dates from July 1929, when fish merchant Christopher William Jordan, of St Andrew's Dock, secured the contract to supply the whole of the fish required for the Boy Scouts World Jamboree held in Birkenhead. The 'wet fish fillets' went in two deliveries over two weeks, of 4.5 to 5 tons each. The lorry is parked outside their works at Billingsgate, on the dock, where they had been located since c.1904. Mr Jordan died in 1941, but his company continued to trade until c.1975. On the rear of this promotional postcard Mr Jordan gives a list of his many achievements, under the title 'undeniable facts', including:

'I was the Pioneer of Filleting, it is now the largest part of the Fishing Industry. I was the originator of the Direct to Consumer distribution scheme, and cheap fish can now be obtained by the working classes in any part of the country. I was the originator of the Small Box System, now taken up by many here (for proof apply N.E.R. Rly Co.), over one million boxes are railed weekly. 10,000 workers being found employment, all through my distribution schemes'.

Three-Wheeled Van • William Craft was listed in the trade directories as a draper and hosier in Myton from c.1872, his son formed Fred J Craft & Co in 1885, and his father joined him in business three years later. In 1905 it became a limited company as William Craft & Sons. Several large stores were spread across the city, and the company continued – latterly with a much-reduced number of premises – until 1942, when the company went into voluntary liquidation. Shown here is another vehicle with a body built by Annison's. The three-wheel vehicles were commonly available from c.1904, and made available initially by the Riley Cycles Company.

Crafts' Ltd clearly found it a useful city runabout as an addition to their fleet. The six horse-power Cyclone Tricar shown above, with a green van-body, was registered to them in January 1912.

The clumsy extended motorcycle handlebars were soon replaced on three-wheelers with a steering-wheel. Later versions were known as Tri-Vans, and continued to be used until the 1960s. Three-wheelers for social and pleasure use were also available and developed into the well-known 'Bubble-car' and Bond Bug, and of course the very popular Reliant Robins, Regals etc.

Motorcycles • As early as 1901 The East Riding Cycle & Motor Co, of Grosvenor Street in Hull, were advertising:

'HIGH-GRADE CYCLES, MOTOR WAGGONETTES, VOITURES, QUADRICYCLES, TRICYCLES, and MOTOR BICYCLES. — Your own Machine fitted with 1½ h.p. Motor, complete, £25; Motor Bicycles, 1½ h.p. any fittings, 35 guineas, complete. Sole agents for the celebrated 6½ h.p. "LIBERIA" VOITURETTE, to seat four.'

Also in 1901 Donsworth Brothers of Prince's Road were advertising: '

Motor Bicycles built to order; come and see samples running' ...
'Motor Tricycle, two-speed gear, and two-seated trailer; cheap for cash'.

Motor driven bicycles had been around since the 1880s, but it was not until c.1900 that they were commonly available and reliable.

Top-left opposite is a Minerva Motorcycle with no plate, so must date from pre-1904. Top-right are staff and family of cycle manufacturers Brown Brothers, with a 3.5 horse-power BSA motorcycle registration AT93, first registered in May 1914. At the bottom of the opposite page is another example of a Hull registered bike with the tell-tale 'AT' plate; AT426, a 3.5 horse-power Triumph, was first registered in February 1907.

Above is AT439, first registered in March 1907 to plumber Tom Cross of 231 Anlaby Road – a 3.5 horse-power Rex motorcycle.

Motorcycle Meeting • This image dates from c.1919, and shows a group of motorcycles and 'light vehicles' outside the City Hotel & Restaurant, opposite the Guildhall. This was almost certainly the annual rally of the Hull Auto Cycle & Light Vehicle Club (originally the Hull & East Riding Auto Cycle Club) to Bleak House at Patrington, held in June that year, which set off from outside the Guildhall. Many of those gathered were no doubt dressed in Burberry motorcycle coats, available from as early as 1904, from their agent in Hull, Hammonds, who were then in Osborne Street. Formed in 1906, the club had their first annual dinner at the Grosvenor Hotel in Carr Lane in November 1907. Another club, the East Yorkshire Motor Cycling Club was formed at a meeting held in the Cross Keys pub on Beverley Road in May 1912. Mr T H Straker, the organiser, had previously been the secretary of the Hull Auto Cycle Club. The new was to have its headquarters in Hull, with affiliations to the RAC and the Auto Cycle Union.

Motorcycle Trip • Seen here around 1910, at the corner of Beverley Road and Cottingham Road – outside the original Haworth Arms, are probably members of the Hull Auto & East Riding Auto Cycle Club. In August 1909 the club held many 'reliability tests', which set off from the Haworth Arms at 2:30 pm, taking a route via Beverley, Driffield and Bridlington; returning via Carnaby, Lissett, Beeford, Brandesburton, Leven, Long Riston, Skirlaugh, Coniston, Sutton, Stoneferry and Newland. Other events held by the club included 'speed trails' (often to Hornsea), social runs, and 'hill climbs' – mostly held around South Cave. The club survived into the 1950s at least, although it had been known as the Hull Auto Cycle & Light Car Club since c.1919. Several motorbike clubs and societies have existed in the intervening years and in 2015 the Hull & District Motor Cycle Club holds regular meetings, events, and an annual family camp.

Stoneferry Bus • Seen here parked in Ann Watson Street, Stoneferry in 1909, is one of six Saurer omnibuses purchased by Hull City Tramways. The buses were supplied by the Mersey Railway Company of Birkenhead. Residents of Wilmington and Stoneferry had long complained that they had no tram service, and a motor bus service between North Bridge and Stoneferry Green began in July 1909. The Hull Daily Mail reported that: 'a capital smoking concert was given at the Grapes Hotel to commemorate the commencement of the service'. At the annual Stoneferry & District Amateur Gardeners Society in August 1909, some councillors arrived half an hour late on the new bus: 'because of delays at the many level crossings and bridges', one remarking that: 'if you want to go to Stoneferry you have to walk'. Despite its overall popularity the service was withdrawn on 5 April 1912, allegedly due to high maintenance costs, and it was not until the 1920s (see opposite) that Stoneferry had another bus service to the city.

Stoneferry Bus • The bus shown above dates from the inauguration of a 1921 service from Bond Street to Stoneferry Green, via Charles Street and Barmston Street. It is parked outside the old Hammond's building in Jameson Street that was demolished following blitz damage in the Second World War. From Jameson Street the bus went to its terminus in Bond Street. Shown left is another of the corporation's early buses being inspected on the Corporation Field in Park Street. This was one of three double-deckers on Bristol chassis, that were supplied to Hull Corporation Tramways in 1923, with bodywork by Dick Kerr, tram manufacturers of Preston.

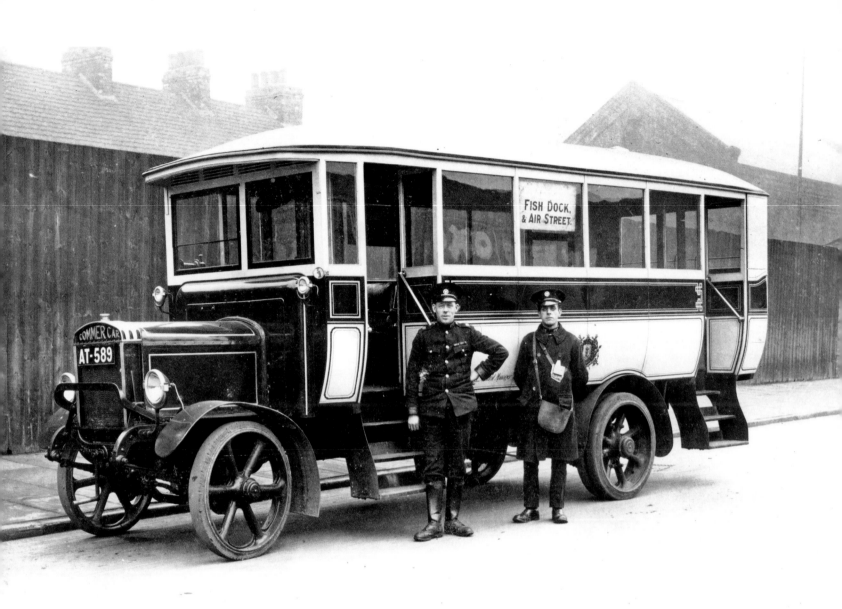

Fish Dock Bus • An article in the Hull Daily Mail of 29 September 1909, entitled 'Not Wanted on Hessle Road', reported the views aired at a 'lively ratepayers' meeting', noting:

> 'Cold water—icy cold water—was dashed at the suggestion made by Mr W. G. Smith at Tuesday night's meeting of the Hull Coltman and Albert Ward's Ratepayers' Association, that it was desirable to have a system of motor 'buses from the Fish Dock ...'

Despite this, a service was eventually introduced in 1923, from the Fish Dock via Queen Victoria Square, to Air Street and still poorly-served Stoneferry. Controversy reigned over the route however, when in 1930 passengers complained this was one of very few where children had to pay a penny to travel, rather than a halfpenny on other routes. By 1928 Hull had 32 motor buses on the road (and still 180 trams) serving the over 67 million passengers that the corporation carried in that year alone.
The bus shown above dates from the late 1920s.

Bus Outing • The buses above are parked alongside what we now call the New Theatre in Jarratt Street. The occasion was the 'Hull Corporation Tram & Bus Workers Effort for Hull's Poor Kiddies outing to Hornsea' in August 1934. Over 400 children were taken away for the day, and on arrival each was given sixpence to spend and a small carrier containing fruit and toys. Donkey rides were given during the day and 'dinner and tea' were supplied at the Unity Hall. Shown left are some of the staff and volunteers that made the day happen.

The bus at the front, registration KH6239, was a 56-seater Bristol, first registered in March 1929, which remained in service until 1943.

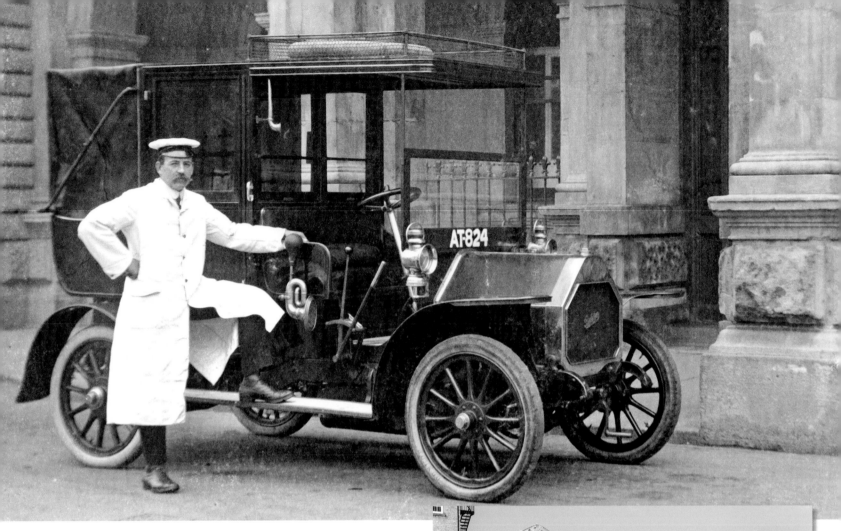

Taxicab • The name taxi is shortened from taxicab, derived from the two words taximeter and cabriolet. The taximeter, invented in 1891, is used to record distances and calculate a fare, and cabriolet originally referred to a horse-drawn carriage where the driver stood at the rear of the carriage. The first documented use of the word taxicab is thought to have been in March 1907 in London. From 1908 to 1909 the number of licensed 'motor cabs' in England increased from 1,508 to 3,394 and became serious competition for the Hansom cabs and four-wheeled cabs. By 1910 there were 20 cab proprietors listed in the Hull directory, of which just two were advertising as motor-cabs; George Richardson, and Thomas Foden Hewer of Alexandra Road. Shown above, alongside the Station Hotel, is a Belsize taxicab, first registered in 1910 to cab proprietor George Richardson. Taxicabs still gather outside the Paragon Station, under where once was the original porte-cochère that was removed in 1962.

The 'question of taxicabs for Hull' was first discussed in 1908 and drew immediate criticism from the established horse-drawn hackney-carriage cab-men. In February 1908, following a news report that a London firm had requested a licence to bring 50 'taximeter-cabs' to Hull, a local cab-man expressed his views in the Mail:

> 'Sir,—I noticed in your Monday's issue remarks as to the havoc proposed taxi-cabs will play amongst the hackney carriage drivers of this city. I, as a citizen and also a cabman, would like to substantiate this. The cabbing of this city at the present time is a hand-to-mouth fight, and apparently, at a later stage, it will mean the workhouse for many.'

The matter was further discussed and the first taxicabs were on the streets of Hull in October that year, 'attracting a great deal of curiosity'. The first taxi firms operating cabs in Hull did little to endear themselves to the public however, as several drivers were prosecuted for speeding (over the 13 mph taxicab limit) and driving dangerously; one 'smash' resulted in a taxicab running into a hackney carriage, running over the horse, which subsequently had to be shot. The local manager of the Provincial Motor Cab Co, who were licensed for the first ten taxicabs in Hull in October 1908, went to print to apologise for the conduct of his drivers. He was moved to impose 'more stringent regulations' upon them following more Police Court proceedings in December 1908, again for excessive speeding.

The main reason for the public's and existing hackney carriage men's complaints centred around the fact that the first companies allowed taxicabs in Hull were national – not local. Hackney carriage proprietor George Richardson, who had been in business at least 20 years, was one of the early complainants. He voiced the concerns of many regarding the Corporation rates and other charges that he and his local colleagues paid, whereas the 'foreigners' paid none. Mr Richardson was one of, if not the first, to bring his own taxicabs to his fleet at his Station Stables from 1910 (see opposite). A new taxicab stand was placed outside the Paragon Station, near to the Station Hotel; horse-cabs allocated five stands, and taxicabs five also. The first standard fare for a ride in a taxicab was six-pence for the first half mile, plus two-pence for each succeeding sixth of a mile.

Motorised wagonettes had been on the streets of Hull for some years when the taxicabs arrived, the first being a Daimler wagonette in 1903. However it was soon taken off the road, as horses 'took fright' when it passed by. Above is a late 1920s image showing part of the fleet of David Burn's local motor coach company 'Grey De-Luxe' fleet. Based in Albert Avenue, the company continued into the 1950s. KH8886 was a Ford, first registered in 1925, KH-7091 was an Associated Daimler, 32-seater in grey of course, first registered in June 1928. KH4071 was a Leyland 31-seater, registered in Februaury 1927; this coach was taken by the War Department in 1940, for use in the Second World War, and following damage was scrapped in 1944.

TELEPHONE CENTRAL 4842,
.CHARABANCS AND BUSES FOR PRIVATE TOURS OF ANY DISTANCE
UNDERTAKEN, APPLY THE MANAGEMENT,
NEWINGTON MOTOR & ENGINEERING Cᵒ, Lᵀᴰ
53. WALTON STREET, HULL.

Charabancs • A motor charabanc was established on runs around the East Yorkshire seaside towns by the North Eastern Railway Co, from August 1905, and in October 1906 an 'enterprising young man' was running another from Paragon Station to the Hull Fair.

In the years leading up to the First World War motor charabancs became a regular sight around Hull, and in July 1914 the Hull & East Riding Garage, 165 Anlaby Road, promoted their 'newly purchased luxurious motor char-a-banc, to seat 35, to let on hire for parties at reasonable terms'. By September that year they were offering weekly trips to Welton or Swanland, and several 20 mile 'country runs' for a shilling and three pence.

Seen here is a later proprietor, the Newington Motor & Engineering Co, of 'Red Triangle Garage', 53 Walton Street. This company first appeared in 1919 inviting 'all owners of motor cycles, cars, lorries and steam waggons … when requiring repairs or renewals'. In 1920 they were granted a licence to run charabancs 'over the districts roads'. This they did, establishing regular runs to Hornsea, and remained in business until c.1930.

Amongst the vehicles shown here is AT-7373, complete with the Newington Motors monogram on its side, which was a 25 horse-power Crossley 14-seater, first registered in 1916. The bodywork was red, white and gold initially, with black guards.

Toffee Works Outing • Grey Cars was a subsidiary of Riley's Dairies of Campbell Street in Hull, formed in 1920, and by March that year was taking Hull supporters to the NU Cup semi-final at Wigan for a return fare of 20 shillings. In 1923 the company noted the 'unprecedented success' of motor tours around the Lake District, claiming that Grey Cars 'originated these long tours', and 'give the highest satisfaction'. A six-day motor tour to Scotland would cost just £48/10s, all inclusive, and the Lakeland four-day trip just over £8/8s. Grey Cars continued in business until 1926.

A Grey Cars' solid-wheeled Albion charabanc is shown here, overflowing with staff from the Steam Toffee Works of William Clayton around 1922. William Clayton was first listed as a wholesale confectioner in West Parade in 1900, and by 1905 had a shop nearby on Spring Bank. In 1906 he moved to premises in Walker Street off the south side of Anlaby Road. Sadly it was here that in 1909 he was fined for employing children below the age of 12. It is the Walker Street factory that is shown here, where Clayton's remained until 1930, when the company went into liquidation.

Reckitt & Sons Charabanc • A charabanc body was fitted to this Bristol delivery lorry belonging to Reckitt & Sons, shown here outside the Francis Reckitt Institute c.1923; probably one of many company vehicles taking staff to Southcoates Station for their annual trip. Reckitts were known for their excellent staff social care, and annual outings became a regular event from the late 1900s. Their 1906 outing to Scarborough saw 2,800 ticket holders leave Southcoates Station on four trains. As was the custom, the director Thomas Ferens, his wife, and other senior staff travelled with the workforce. This vehicle was almost new at the time of the photograph, having been first registered in July 1922. A four-ton Bristol 'rully & charabanc', it was coloured 'Royal Blue' according to its registration record.

Work on the Francis Reckitt Institute began in 1915, replacing an older facility, but building work was delayed by the First World War. In 1916 for example, three of the men engaged in ferro-concrete construction on the site were refused dispensation from enlistment; the firm had 50 men working on the job at the time, but only 10 were of 'military age' including those three. The institute was in use by March 1919, and was damaged by enemy action during the Second World War in 1941. It was rebuilt in 1949 and further upgraded in 1979. As I write in September 2015 the 100-year-old Institute is being demolished for a new research and development facility.

Ambulance • It was 1915 before Hull requested its own motor ambulances, councillors visiting suppliers with a view to purchasing the first two in May that year. The Health Committee had its first motor ambulance in May 1917 (AT1202) built by Alldays (supplied by Wilson & Stockwell); having suffered a broken stub axle in May 1928, it was transferred to the Public Cleansing Committee in July 1928 and converted to a dust cart. This was followed by an Atlas (AT6517) in February 1922, supplied by the Central Motor Mart in Hull, but this was wrecked in an accident in November 1928 and scrapped.

Additionally, the Watch Committee also had ambulances for the Police Force, the first – a converted Ford – was registered in May 1920 (AT3053) followed by a Dennis (AT9808) that was purchased new in September 1924. A fully-equipped ambulance costs well over £250,000 in 2015, whereas the first ambulances purchased in Hull cost around of £600.

The ambulance shown above outside the old Prospect Street Infirmary, seated six patients under canvass (if they were able), in a body that was fitted to a Daimler 20 h.p. chassis, painted deep blue.

Hull Police Fire Brigade Pump-Escape Engine • Seen in front of the original Jarratt Street elevation of the Hull Fire Station in Worship Street, is vehicle registration AT5946, a 1921 model Dennis N-Type pump-escape. This was the second pump-escape acquired by Hull, and was delivered on 21 March 1921 (Dennis delivery records, Surrey History Centre) and had a Bayley 50-foot, wheeled escape ladder. Hand-operated, the ladder was capable of reaching five storeys. Seen not long after delivery, the chap in dungaree-fatigues looks as though he is about to re-align the offside headlight, which appears to be sitting at an odd angle. This vehicle was transferred to East Hull sometime after the station opened there, and was used for war work from 1941, and transferred back to the Hull Fire Brigade ownership in September 1948. It was numbered 3, as it was the third motor fire engine (not the third pump-escape) acquired by the Hull Fire Brigade.

The urgent need for motor fire engines in Hull had been voiced in the press for several years prior to Hull's first motor fire engine being authorised, a Leyland purchased in 1915. On 14 July 1915 the Hull Watch Committee; Fire Brigade Sub-Committee reported that they had:

> '... ordered from Leyland Motor (1914) Ltd., a six-cyclinder 600 gallons large motor fire engine with fittings, at a cost of £1,370, and a 400 gallons Leyland Standard motor fire engine with 50ft. wheeled escape, first aid pumps, 13in. gong, etc., at a cost of £1,295, both engines to be delivered complete to Hull.'

An article in the Hull Daily in December 1915 detailed a 'first-look' at the initial engine, and the writer described how 'remarkably robust' the vehicle was: 'as it needs to be with a dozen or more firemen hanging on to it on the way to a fire'. The second engine arrived in 1916.

Empress Hotel, Alfred Gelder Street, as re-built in 1903. The architect J.H. Hirst stood outside.

Chapter Three
Pubs

For Graham

Barmston Hotel, Barmston Street • Barmston Street, originally known as Cotton Mill Street (from its close proximity to the Kingston Cotton Mill in nearby Cumberland Street), was re-named c.1863 when a new estate of streets was laid out on land formerly occupied by the 'Prince Albert Strawberry Gardens', one of several large pleasure gardens in this area. Pubs were often the first buildings to appear in these new developments, as they were commonly used by the employer to pay wages, and as a site office. Thus the **Barmston Inn** was established on the corner of Barmston Street and Lincoln Street c.1869, the first landlord being George Eccles, and was owned by brewer William Glossop whose Imperial Brewery was at that time nearby in Lincoln Street. Details from the annual Brewster Sessions in the Hull Packet newspaper of 26 August 1870 noted that the inn had transferred from Mr Eccles to the next tenant:

'Mr Leake supported an application for a licence for the **Barmston Inn**, 71 Barmston Street, occupied by John Simpson Richardson and owned by William Glossop. He presented a memorial signed by approximately 250 residents in the neighbourhood. Mr Iveson jun., opposed on behalf of Mr Henry Wilson of the Kingston Hotel, Cumberland-street.'

The Barmston received its first 'six-day' licence in 1874, although it had been trading since its construction c.1869, and was first listed in the trade directories as 71 Barmston Street, but by 1879 had been renumbered as 88. As was commonplace for larger pubs with 'club-rooms' over the premises, the Barmston Hotel was home to at least one lodge of a friendly society. The 'Thomas Witty Lodge (no.620) of the G.U.O. Oddfellows' held its meetings here in the 19th century, frequently attended by 100 members or more. Glossop's pubs were taken over by the Hull Brewery Co in 1920, and it is just a few years after that date that the photograph opposite was taken; note three doors leading to three separate drinking areas including a 'Dram Shop'. The name board over the door reveals that Eva Simmonite was the tenant, her late husband having been at the pub since 1900; Eva remained until the mid-1930s. The photograph top-left – made from the same vantage point, just outside St Silas' church gates – was taken in the 1960s. By that time the pub had been stripped of its Victorian decoration, original windows, gas-lamp bracket etc, and had been rendered in the bland style that was common after the Second World War. After a century of trading, the pub closed c.1970 as the housing in this area was cleared under compulsory purchase, and was demolished shortly after, the site remaining empty today.

John Wyles

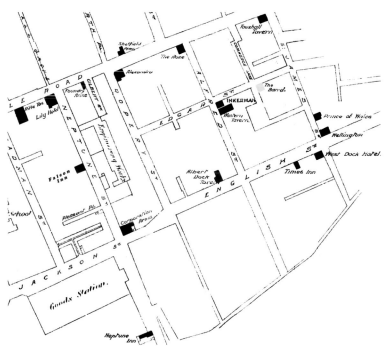

Barrel Tavern, Edgar Street • This compact tavern was established when the area known as Myton, south of the present Hessle Road, spread west as the population of the town of Hull grew beyond the Old Town walls. It was in the heart of a smaller area known as the 'Pottery', after the potteries that were situated nearby on the Humber Bank. This area was also known as English Town, an area developed around the new church of St James, as the land here was mostly owned by Hull merchant Thomas English; Edgar Street, laid out in 1802, was named after Edgar Wilkins English, his youngest son. One of the earliest Hull trade directories – Battle's 1803 – notes just four inhabitants in the new street – two chandlers, a cordwainer and a baker, but no pub. Situated on the south side of the narrow street, at the entrance to St Mark's Square, the **Barrel Tavern** first opened c.1810, with William Sawyer noted as the first victualler. By 1814 a change of tenant reveals its first noted address as 8 Edgar Street, later expanding to take in the house next door, and re-numbered as 7. From c.1848, as the street filled with new properties, it became 17, and much later 80, which it remained.

At the left of the original tavern frontage can be seen the entrance to Barrel Court. Containing just three cramped dwellings the court was later demolished to enable a single-storey extension at the side of the pub. Although the pub closed some time in the early 1980s, thankfully the building has been preserved. In an area that remains densely packed with industrial premises, the former tavern has been home to a variety of small cafe businesses, serving breakfast and lunch to the workforce as it does in 2015 – and now known as Aunt Sally's.

The images show the pub c.1926 (opposite page), just after closure (top-left), and on an early 20th century map (above), which also shows the many other pubs that were in the immediate area.

"BIRD IN HAND" INN HULL F.N.PETTINGELL ARCH

OFFICE AND KINGSTON WORKS, HULL, *from th*

Bird In Hand Inn, Dansom Lane • In August 1851 the Hull Packet newspaper contained details of the annual Brewster Sessions in which:

'Mr Mathew Baron sought a licence for the **Bird in the Bush**, Dansom-lane, and was supported by Mr Russel from the office of Mr E Wilson.'

This appears to be the first reference to the beer-house that became known as the **Bird in Hand**, although it is very likely from entries in the trade directories that the small beer-house was established perhaps 10 years earlier. It was almost certainly built on the site of one of Dansom Lane's original three windmills. The Reckitt family had begun their business on land adjacent to the building around 1840, and that would seem an appropriate date for anyone wishing to establish a pub in the area. The 1851 census records reveal that 43 year-old Mathew was born in Wigan, as were his family of five daughters, one son and his wife Betty – all present at the pub on the night of the census. By 1876 the pub had been taken over by Hewitt Brothers brewery of Grimsby, and it was they who rebuilt it 1876-77, as shown in the drawing by architect Frank Pettingell shown opposite. As shown in the c.1905 photograph top-left, and the early 1920s aerial photograph top-right, the Reckitt & Colman factories had expanded hugely, taking in all of the land around the over-shadowed pub premises. Reckitts sought constantly to have the licence of the pub removed, as its presence under the boardroom window of the mostly teetotal Reckitt directors had long been a thorn in the company's side. An initial offer of £500 was made in 1909, but the brewery knew they had the upper-hand in the bargaining. After further offers of £5,500 in 1918 and £6,500 in 1921,

it was not until 1923 that they finally succeeded; the pub closed on 2 June that year, having been purchased for £7,500. The old pub buildings were soon removed – as they also stood alongside the Memorial Gardens established by Reckitts c.1920 in honour of those lost in the First World War. The mid-section of Dansom Lane has long been owned (and closed) by the company. As I write in September 2015, demolition is in progress to clear the oldest of the Reckitts buildings adjacent to the Memorial Gardens and the site of the old pub. A large new research & development facility is to be built.

Blacksmiths Arms, Strawberry Street • The 1841 census listed 40 year-old Thomas Price as a 'moulder' living in the Strawberry Gardens, Drypool with his wife and two daughters. An 1842 trade directory listed Thomas Price as an ale & porter dealer at the **Iron Moulders Arms**, Strawberry Lane, Church Street. This was the first reference to the pub that in 1855 became known as the Blacksmiths' Arms, when J Grasby applied for a 'new' licence for premises in 'the Strawberry Gardens, Strawberry-st' according to the Brewster Sessions listed in the Hull Packet newspaper; another 1855 notice had referred to Mr Grasby as being 'of the **Blacksmiths' Arms**, Drypool'.

As the old Strawberry Gardens became fully built upon the pub's regular address evolved as 1 Strawberry Street (originally known as Strawberry Garden Lane) and 35 Naylor's Row.

In 1931 the building was re-fronted by the owner's Darley's Brewery of Thorne, resulting in the appearance we see today. The vaguely neo-Georgian frontage, with multi-pane windows and wide door-casings, was improved by the addition of a fabulous tiled frieze on the corner of the building (replacing the old smoke room entrance door) in the 1960s. This work of art, which depicts Darley's symbol of an armoured horse's head (shown below), is a rare example of its kind (Darley's ceased brewing in 1986). The extension along the Naylor's Row elevation is a modern addition that blends in well. The Excelsior Angling Association met at the pub in the 1890s, and during the 1930s the newly-refurbished premises were headquarters to Newtown R.F.C. (later renamed Excelsior R.F.C.) as well as the usual dominoes and darts teams, and held regular matches in the Hull 'Tip-It' league. Tip-It is a traditional pub game, in which two teams of three face each other across a table and guess in which of the six hands opposite that the item known as the tipit is hidden. Happy days.

It was not until 1957 that the pub received its first full licence, when on the 4 February the licence of the blitz-damaged Grosvenor Hotel (Carr Lane) was surrendered.

The Blacksmiths continues to trade in a tough environment, which is a credit to its tenants past and present. The large photograph opposite shows the pub with regulars around 1910, and the image top-left on this page was taken around 1930.

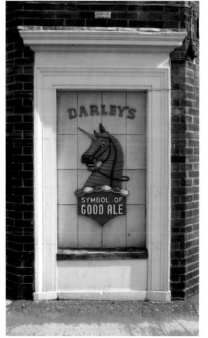

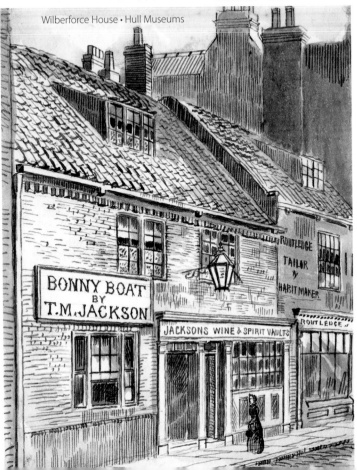

Bonny Boat, Trinity House Lane • The artist Frederick Schultz Smith created the two images on this page in late 1890, providing a valuable record of the old buildings just weeks before they were demolished. Trinity House Lane was first known as part of 'Old Beverley Street', but is recorded in property deeds as 'Sewer-side' in 1591, and by 1644 as 'Trinitie House Lane'. The 'Guild or Fraternity of Masters and Pilots, Seamen of the Trinity House of Kingston upon Hull' – known simply as Trinity House since 1581 – established property on the south side of Whitefriargate in 1461. Trinity House acquired all of the land up to the line of 'Sewer-side', and hence it took the name Trinity House Lane sometime between 1591 and 1644. Hollar's 1640 plan of Hull appears to show a building on the site of the present Bonny Boat pub, and it is possible that this is the building Smith shows here.

The **Bonny Boat** is recorded as a pub in trade directories from 1791, and took its name from an event in 1613, when Captain Andrew Barker, an 'elder brother' of the Trinity House, was at sea in a whaling ship off Greenland. Here he discovered an exhausted local, afloat in a canoe or kayak. Captain Barker took him on board, but he died three days later; his small boat, belongings and clothing were returned to Hull, where they are still on display today in the Trinity House buildings.

At the time of Smith's drawings, the last landlord of the pub had been Thomas Mathew Jackson, who was there from 1880 until c.1890. The old pub was demolished in 1891, and rebuilt as we see it today; its rebuilding was part of a phase of town improvements that also resulted in the construction of the nearby Covered Market Hall in 1902.

The image on the opposite page dates from c.1926 and was taken on behalf of the Hull Brewery Co. It shows in good detail how the rebuilt pub appeared, complete with two decorative tiled panels below the windows, each containing a unique central tile showing the bonny boat with its passengers at sea. Thankfully the pub frontage remains relatively unaltered and it continues to trade to this day.

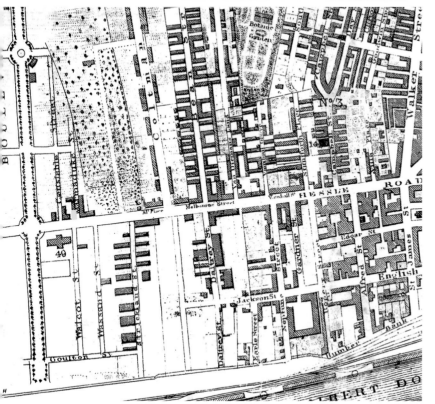

Criterion Hotel, Hessle Road • In August 1874 John Downes applied for an ale-house licence for his recently built premises the 'Criterion Hotel, corner of Marmaduke-st.' Having no opposition, the licence was granted.

This part of Hessle Road was developing rapidly at this time, with new streets in the immediate area being laid out upon land owned by the Constable family – Marmaduke being the son of the Reverend Thomas Constable. The Criterion found itself ideally placed in a central position within this grid development, where other family-related local names included Constable Street, Wassand Street, Goulton Street, Walcott Street and Strickland Street. The pub gave its name (or vice-versa) to the Criterion Cricket Club, whose ground was at the end of the newly-formed Marmaduke Street, and practice ground was in a rented field owned by Mr James Wilson. The club was formed by Mr L Ellis in August 1874 (probably local builder Levens Ellis of Strickland Street) – the same month, and in the same year, that the Criterion was granted a licence. Originally having just 30 members, by December 1875 the club had 175 regulars on its books.

The pub is shown on the opposite page in a c.1926 photograph with 'Iced Lager' for sale, at which time the landlord was James Christopher Battersby, who held the pub from 1920 until the late 1940s. Alongside is a 1920s advertisement; note the pub's telephone number – Central 1830. Top-right on this page is a shot of the pub from 1956. Left is a section of Peck's 1875 plan of Hull showing the location of the new pub, the field used for cricket practice at the end of the street, and the newly developing streets. Still trading in 2015, it is surely one of Hull's more elegant pub frontages.

Steve Ingram Collection

Hull History Centre

Crown & Cushion, Land of Green Ginger • The Crown & Cushion has its origins as two pubs. Situated directly opposite the extant George pub in the Land of Green Ginger, was the Crown & Cushion. First known as the **White Lion**, it was built c.1800 for landlord and coach master Robert Harrison, who ran a coach from Hull to Hessle. It was a large building comprising two front rooms, five lodging (bed) rooms, two garrets and a kitchen. In 1809 it was transferred to William Rickard who was there from 1810 until 1813, and ran the 'Trafalgar Post Coach' from Hull to York and Leeds. In a notice from the Hull Packet of June 1810 he thanked the public for their: 'very liberal encouragement they have so long honoured him with in support of the coach, which will continue to run from his house, the White Lion, in the Land of Green Ginger'.

The **Crown & Cushion** was built c.1790, and entered from a passage at the side of 17 Silver Street just around the corner from the White Lion. This pub was more often referred to simply as 'The Crown' initially – its inn sign being a carved crown upon a cushion, later interpreted as the Crown & Cushion. Martin Cade is the first known victualler, and was there from c.1800 until 1823, when on 6 October the Hull Packet noted a change in owner:

> 'Joseph Ware, Respectfully informs his Friends and the Public in general, that he has taken and entered upon the old established HOUSE, lately rebuilt, and known by the Sign of the CROWN AND CUSHION, in Silver Street, which he has fitted up in a most complete manner for the accommodation of Passengers by the Coaches, Steam Boats, &c. and which he purposes [sic] opening on Thursday the 9th instant. He also begs to inform them that he has laid in a choice and very superior STOCK of WINES, SPIRITUOUS LIQUORS, LONDON BOTTLED and DRAUGHT PORTER.'

Joseph Ware remained at the pub until 1831, at which time the Crown & Cushion, Silver Street, and the White Lion at 3 Land of Green Ginger,

amalgamated under the single name of Crown & Cushion. The White Lion backed onto the Crown & Cushion and presumably one could commute between the two properties via entrances at the rear. The two continued under the name of the Crown & Cushion until 1876 when the Silver Street address was demolished for the construction of the London & Yorkshire Bank (later the National and Provincial Union Bank, and latterly the Nat West buildings). Local brewers Kendall & Gruby had formed a partnership in 1876, when they took over the South Myton Brewery – re-naming it the Exchange Brewery. In 1892 Worthingtons bought the Exchange Brewery and its estate of 24 pubs, which was then broken up. The estate included the Crown & Cushion, Land of Green Ginger, and it is likely that the demolition of the Silver Street building was linked with the sale.

Documents in the Hull City Archives record that the property's owner, ship builder Edward Gibson of Great Union Street, had ... 'added a new front, and the bar has been enlarged and reconstructed into four compartments, each of which have an entrance leading from the passage' ... in 1891.

The Crown & Cushion remained a Worthington's house, and the picture top-right shows the front and the passage entrance (left) just prior to closure. Closing on 3 September 1927, it too was demolished (5 September) for an extension to the bank that had required the demolition of its former partner in Silver Street. The last tenant was William Craig (1925-27). At closure it was one of the few houses in the City with an official singing licence.

The Eastern Morning News of 21 September 1927 carried a notice which read: 'the old sign, which was supposedly made of stone and plaster, has been cleaned and restored, and is now in the Wilberforce Museum'.

The photograph on the opposite page shows Land of Green Ginger from Whitefriargate, and gives an excellent view of the location of the Crown & Cushion, visible in the shade on the right hand side of the street.

DE LA POLE STREET

Duke of Edinburgh, De La Pole Place • The Duke of Edinburgh pub has remained, relatively unchanged externally, in full view of its neighbour over the road – the Victoria Dock Tavern (see book cover) – for around 180 years. No buildings are shown on the site on Anderson's Plan of 1818, but by the time of Greenwood's plan of 1835 De La Pole Place is shown (on the line of De La Pole Street) with buildings on the site of the Duke of Edinburgh. In 1835 Richard Townsley was listed in a trade directory at a beer-house in 'Great Union Street', corrected in later directories to 'De La Pole Place', and named as **The Gate** in an 1838 directory. From 1840 Richard Haswell was landlord, and remained for 50 years; during his tenure the pub's confusing location, which was actually De La Pole Place – a short terrace facing the main street of Garrison Road – was listed variously as Garrison Road, De La Pole Place, De La Pole Street and 1 Great Union Street.

The 1851 census records Richard Haswell at his beer-house, correctly as De La Pole Place, aged 36, and noted as a 'master bricklayer and beer retailer employing four men'. With him were his wife, three sons and a daughter. Clearly a man of standing, he was elected as a guardian of the poor in Sculcoates Union in 1855, and as a builder, built the National School in Drypool in 1863. By the 1871 census Richard had five sons and four daughters, and was also listed as a marine stores dealer in the 1870s.

Richard died in 1890 and from that date, under new landlord James Mumby, the pub was first noted as the **Duke of Edinburgh Hotel**. Again the trade directories confused its address as 1 De La Pole Street, when it is clear from the location of the windows and main frontage that it faces what was originally De La Pole Place. In 2015 it faces 'Citadel Way' although the original granite-sett road surface of Garrison Road/De La Pole Place remains defiantly in view.

This area suffered badly during the bombings of the Second World War, and although St Peter's church opposite was severely damaged, the Duke of Edinburgh survived with just its windows blown in.

The closure of Victoria Dock in 1970 hit the trade of many pubs in this area, but the development of the Victoria Dock housing estate from 1988 helped keep the pubs afloat. Dense industry in the area also provides regular trade, and the pub remains popular as part of the Friday and Saturday night pub-crawls that take in the old and new pubs in this area and along Witham.

The photograph top-left shows the pub in 1955 looking north from De La Pole Street to the ruins of St Peter's church, and the larger image on the opposite page shows it c.1926 – note the small door to the Smoke Room, which survives to this day. The advertisement shown opposite, for Richard Haswell's business, is taken from an 1855 trade directory.

Earl De Grey, Castle Street • Numbers 6, 7 and 8 Castle Street (right to left in these images) were constructed as one building c.1790; at that time this area was still often referred to as 'Myton Gates Without'.

During the 1840s, up until at least 1846, 6 Castle Street was listed as the premises of confectioner Ann Walker, and at 7 was painter J Chapman.

By 1848 the **Junction Dock Inn** was listed at 6 – the first landlord being Sam Tweddell. The 1851 census notes Samuel John Tweddell as a chain-maker and innkeeper at 6 Castle Street (the Junction Dock Tavern is recorded as 6 & 7 Castle Street in an 1851 trade directory), and next door at 8 was a 'coffee-house' run by a Mr Welburn. The Junction Dock Tavern was one of five pubs along this short stretch of road, the others being the Commercial Hotel, Regatta Tavern, Lumper's Arms and the Spread Eagle.

Junction Dock had been proposed as early as 1802, but construction did not commence until 1826, and it opened on 1 June 1829. Following the visit of Queen Victoria and Prince Albert in 1854, it was re-named Prince's Dock. Frederick Robinson, Viscount Goderich, was elected as an MP for Hull in 1852 but was later unseated for dubious electoral practices. He became MP for Huddersfield in 1853, and for the West Riding in 1857, and was appointed to the position of High Steward of Hull in 1863, by which time he had acquired the title of Earl De Grey and Ripon. In 1863-64 the Junction Dock Inn was re-named the **Earl De Grey Tavern**. Numbers 6 & 7 were separated again c.1864-66, when 6 reverted to a shop, and 7 was extended to take in the former coffee-house to the west at 8 (see 1864 plan opposite). The ornate faience-tiled frontage of the pub was probably added during a 1913 renovation by Bentley's Yorkshire Brewery.

The pub narrowly survived demolition in the late 1970s for the present dual-carriageway, and in June and July 1988 the eastern third of the block – half of the original 1848 Junction Dock Inn – was demolished to make way for the Princes Quay development. Prince's Dock had closed to shipping in 1968.

The property was given Grade II listed building status in 1980 during the Mytongate/Castle Street redevelopment scheme, and was saved from demolition due to the high quality of its beautiful tiled facade.

The creation of the dual-carriageway here, and the development of the shopping centre, effectively sealed the fate of the Earl De Grey. The interior of the property has little to show of its former days as the Junction Dock Tavern, but the pub underwent extensive renovation in 2004. Its future remains in doubt

sadly, as does that of Castle Street's other listed buildings further west – Castle Buildings, and the attached shop. As with the old town properties south of the lumbering new roadway, it has become 'out of the way', and difficult to access, with no decent ways of crossing for pedestrians. The pub has recently been closed more often than open, and has remained boarded-up since 2010. With work soon to begin on a proposed new Ferensway and Castle Street junction, I suspect the building will be lost. I hope the unique exterior is preserved, even if reconstructed elsewhere, but it seems unlikely. The Earl De Grey is shown on the opposite page c.1950, and top-right in my photograph from the mid-1980s, when all of the original building still survived. The floor-plan above is re-drawn from an 1864 document.

Elephant & Castle, Holderness Road • An ale-house licence was granted in August 1873 for: 'Mr Robert Massam's public house on the corner of Garbutt Street and Holderness Road, the **Elephant & Castle**.' Robert's new pub was one of three pubs in Hull that have held this name, the others being in Mytongate in the early 19th century, and another in High Street from the 1830s to c.1860. In October 1875 he was also granted a licence to sell spirits, wine and sweets 'off the premises'. It was not until 1877 that a six-day licence was granted, when that of the Hope & Anchor in Bishop Lane was transferred.

Barnsley Street was initially named Garbutt Street when first laid out c.1870, after the developer David Garbutt (see Hull Then & Now 3, chapter one) but was renamed Barnsley Street c.1882. The new name was a reference to the new high-level railway line of the Hull & Barnsley Railway, constructed close-by in 1881. The street was mentioned by name in an announcement for the rugby club Hull Southcoates, who played a benefit match: 'in a field opposite Barnsley Street', in September that year. The pub's address was also recorded as 1 Albion Parade, which was the terrace of property it adjoined, all facing Holderness Road, but later numbered 247 Holderness Road as the area became fully-developed.

Around 1936 the beautiful old frontage was lost during the redevelopment of the building, which resulted in that we see today; the adjacent shop on Holderness Road was taken in during the rebuilding. In 1937 the Elephant & Castle received its first full seven-day licence, when the Carpenters Arms in Great Union Street surrendered its licence.

The pub suffered some damage during the Second World War, when at least three high-explosive bombs were dropped around it in May 1941; the damage didn't close the pub however, as it was reported in the Hull Daily Mail of 17 November 1943 that the landlord had been fined for 'blackout offences'. It was also actively seeking 'full-time experienced barmaids' in the Hull Daily Mail in 1944.

The photograph opposite dates from c.1900, and that shown top-right from 1956. At the time of writing the pub has been closed for some time.

Observe!
FLOWER POT,
63,
WHITEFRIARGATE

GIN! GIN!

PRIME, only 10s. per gallon ; | Cordialised, only 6s. 8d. per gallon
1s. 3d. per pint. | 10d. per pint.
Spirit of Gin, 12s. per gallon ; | Gin, 8s. per gallon ; 1s. per pint.
1s. 6d. per pint.

Fine XXX ALE, 4d. per Quart.
Best LONDON PORTER, 3½d. per Quart.

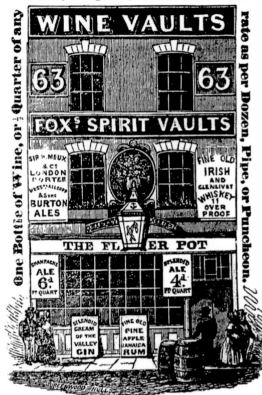

FAMILY WINE AND SPIRIT VAULTS,
FLOWER POT, 63, WHITEFRIARGATE, HULL.

THIS ESTABLISHMENT IS SURPASSED BY NONE IN ENGLAND FOR CHEAPNESS
AND QUALITY.

THE IMMENSE STOCK the Proprietor does, with confidence, recommend to his numerous
Friends, which consists of several Hundred Dozens fine old and well-matured rich PORT and SHERRY

WINES,

With a corresponding Stock of HOCK, SPARKLING CHAMPAGNE, MADEIRA, LISBON, TENT,
BUCELLAS, MARSALA, &c. &c.; and a well-known Stock of both

FOREIGN AND BRITISH SPIRITS,

Namely fine pale old

BRANDY,

Warranted of the Vintage of 1820, and other Brandies ; fine GENEVA as imported ; splendid Pine Apple

JAMAICA RUM

Unrivalled

LONDON GIN,

Drawn from the Distiller's Cask ; genuine Mont Blairy, Glenury, and Small-Still, Eleven Over-Proof, and

REAL IRISH WHISKIES,

Warranted 20 per Cent. Over Proof, &c., &c.; and 1,125 Dozens of Sir H. Meux and Co.'s superior

LONDON PORTER.

A List of Prices to be had at the Establishment.   OBSERVE The Establishment 63 Whitefriargate, Hull.

Flower Pot, Whitefriargate • Previously in the occupation of hairdresser Mr Brooks, 63 Whitefriargate became the **Anchor** beer-house c.1809 with the first victualler being Robert Hunt. Mr Hunt was jailed for bankruptcy charges in 1835, and shortly after the pub was renamed the **Flower Pot Inn** under Esther Staveley, who remained just a year.

Around 1838 Charles Fox took over and established a well-known wines & spirits business from the premises, retaining the Flower Pot name as shown by the contemporary advertisements opposite, which first appeared in the press c.1841. Fox was bankrupt by 1846 and the premises (advertised as a 'Tavern and Wine Vaults') sold at auction, then becoming known as the **Apollo Tavern** for just one year.

From c.1848 George Wilde Evans was proprietor – also the licensee of the City of London Arms in Lowgate, the site of the present City Hotel. As 'Wilde & Evans' he changed the Flower Pot to the **City Arms** in the 1860s, and later the **City of London Arms**. The pub was rebuilt around this time in the neo-classical Italianate Gin Palace style, one of the first designs of Hull's most famous architect Cuthbert Brodrick. It was re-named the **Flower Pot** once again from c.1868, and it was in that year the local press noted that Mr W Hall of the 'Flower Pot Vaults' took the New Holland Ferry and rode to London. The journey took just three days, on a Penny Farthing bicycle manufactured by the Beverley Iron & Waggon Co.

During the 1890s Thomas Inkson took the premises, and wanting to make his mark changed the name slightly to the **Royal Flower Pot**, which it remained. Although tied to Allsopp's in the 1890s, it became a Hull Brewery house from the early 20th century. It ceased trading on 15 July 1922, when its licence was transferred to the Polar Bear on Spring Bank.

The building was then taken over by Price the Tailors of Leeds, becoming the 'Thirty-five Shilling Tailor' in the 1920s, and the 'Fifty Shilling Tailor' in the 1930s. The striking 1860s arched entrance with classical columns was lost at that point and the shop front seen in the photograph top-left was applied. The whole building, including the remaining Italianate upper floor windows was finally lost in 1956-57, for a clumsy extension to the British Home Stores shop next door; this was the date for the photograph, which shows the demolition company board in the vacant window. The once symmetrical Art-deco/Moderne frontage of the 1934 British Home Stores building was extended out to the left in the same 1930s style as the original building – the join remaining visible to this day.

The construction of the British Home Stores building in 1934 had itself required the demolition of the much larger, 250 year-old, George Hotel. The 'tap' and rear coach entrance of the George Hotel remains in Land of Green Ginger, long-known as the George pub.

Latterly (since c.1990) the site of the former Flower Pot Inn has formed one half of a branch of Super Drug.

Four In Hand, Holderness Road • In an 1840 directory Henry Rogerson is listed at the **Four Alls Inn**, Sutton Ings. Although probably established much earlier, 1840 seems to be the first year that this roadside inn was mentioned by name. Originally titled the Four Alls, the light-hearted inn-sign for pubs of this name was usually made up of four panels – the first showing the Sovereign (I rule all), a Parson (I pray for all), a Soldier (I fight for all) and the last a picture of a working class fellow (I pay for all). During the 1840s the landlord was Richard Baxter, listed in trade directories c.1848 as: 'Richard Baxter corn miller and victualler, Four Alls, Holderness Road'. An 1861 sale notice for the property noted:

'TO BE SOLD AT AUCTION,

LOT 1. All that DWELLING HOUSE and the said PUBLIC HOUSE, known by the name of "The Four Alls", with the Out-buildings, Yard, and the Appurtenances thereto belonging.

LOT 2. All those THREE several COTTAGES or TENEMENTS contiguous to Lot 1.

LOT 3. All that CLOSE or parcel of LAND, also situate at Sutton aforesaid, containing Four Acres and a Half, more or less.

LOT 4. All that PARCEL of GROUND called Wind Mill Plot, with the WIND CORN MILL erected thereupon, and with the Machinery, Tackling, &c belonging thereto. The Mill is in good working order.

The Property is situate on the Hull and Holderness Road, about Three Miles from Kingston-upon-Hull. The Inn has recently been enlarged and thoroughly repaired, and has long been a good-accustomed Inn.'

The pub was again up for auction in 1869, with the windmill still in good working order, described as having a 'very extensive frontage to Sutton Lane'. During the 1880s the Hull Harriers running club ran from here, and in the 1890s it was home to several 'pigeon flying' teams. Late in 1889 the pub was referred to as the **Four In Hand** for the first time in the newspapers, the new name referring to a team of four horses used to pull heavier vehicles.

Sutton Lane, also known as Four Alls Lane, was re-named Bellfield Avenue c.1926 (from the old Belle Field close or field) when new housing estates appeared along Holderness Road; it was mentioned by name in a news report in April 1926. Part of the suburban development that included Bellfield Avenue was for a new and larger Four In Hand Hotel (rebuilt in a style that was older than the original building). It was not until May 1937 that it was reported to be nearing completion, one of three 'new' pubs planned for East Hull (the Lambwath and the Ganstead being the others). There was criticism in the press, home-owners claiming the pubs would affect the value of their new homes. On 22 June 1937 (at 2 pm) an auction of the old: 'Public House Fixtures, Fittings, Trade Utensils Etc', was held at the newly built pub, the notice informing readers that: 'the new house opens 11 am this day!' A later article in July 1937 informed that the old inn sign had been presented to the Wilberforce House Museum, for the 'old street' there. The image above left dates from c.1905, and opposite from c.1937 taken just before demolition; below is a section of the 1890 Ordnance Survey plan showing the pub facing Holderness Road, and the windmill still in place.

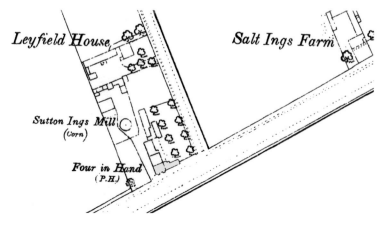

George & Dragon, High Street • A series of papers in the Hull History Centre relating to the ownership of the land on which this pub stood, record an early feoffment (a grant of ownership of freehold property) relating to a 'messuage in High Street, near the Horse Staithe'. It was transferred from 'Hull Corporation' to a beer-brewer named as Stephen Purstwad for £100, and this is possibly the earliest note of the **George & Dragon**, although it was not until 1803 that it was recorded by name in the trade directories.

As High Street is numbered consecutively, the ancient pub was recorded as 101 and 102 High Street, and was on the north-west side of the street where the numbers 'turn around' to carry on back up to the north end.

Various references exist to confirm that a small brewery was located on the premises, as in 1825 the pub was to let 'with brewery utensils in good order'. Again in 1837 and 1842 landlord Thomas Youill was also noted as a brewer on the premises.

In 1882 German-born Charles Stritt and his wife Augusta took over the pub and soon established it as a venue for lager beer. The Stritts had been in Hull since the 1860s and had held licences at three other pubs, including the nearby Brotherton Tavern at 82 High Street. As the advertisement below shows, not only did the George & Dragon serve lager on the premises but also to the trade and general public – 'on reasonable terms'. The exterior of the pub is clearly marked in both photographs with 'Deutsches Gasthaus' (German Inn), as well as the main signboard at roof level that states 'Lager Beer Saloon'.

In January 1908 during an ongoing purge of pubs in the Old Town, 16 pubs were referred for closure and compensation, including six High Street premises; the George Yard Inn, Globe, Lion & Key, Old Harbour, Tigress and the George & Dragon. Four were closed, including the George & Dragon, which held a full alehouse licence. In 1909 £1,108 was agreed in compensation to the owner Mr John W Harrison. It is shown opposite and left during the tenure of Augusta Stritt (Charles died in 1898), who remained the licensee until her death in 1905. The building survived until the 1920s, when it was demolished, and the site has remained empty ever since.

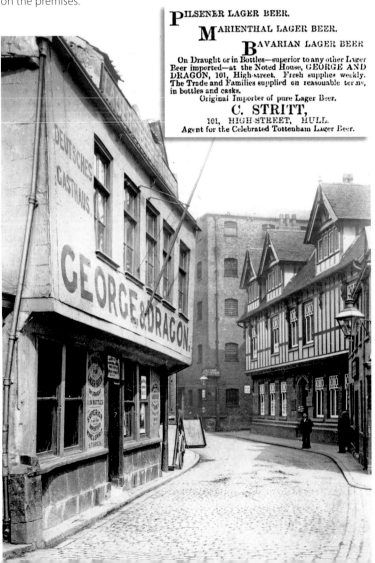

The Grand, George Street • Shopkeeper David Bancroft moved from 44 Chariot Street in 1860 to take new premises at 11 George Street. The 1861 census records him there curiously as a 'Register Office & Waiter', along with his wife who was listed as a confectioner, and their three daughters. Contemporary 1860s trade directories list him simply as a greengrocer & confectioner.

At this date the north side of George Street was a long terrace of houses and shops, interspersed with the odd entrance through to court housing behind. Numbered consecutively from Grimston Street back to Savile Street, 11 and 12 were divided by the passage entrance to a courtyard later in the century known as Norman's Court. By the time of the 1871 census David Bancroft was recorded as a newsagent & beer-retailer, still at 11 with his wife, and three daughters – one listed as a 'stewardess' by this time. It seems Mr Bancroft had chosen to open a beer-house at a very fortuitous time, as George Street was already home to several Music Halls, Gentlemen's Clubs, and 'Turkish Baths'. Number 13 – the four-bay property adjacent – was Fussey's Music Hall in the early 1870s, but taken over by brewer Joseph Bentley in the 1880s. The grand Georgian street was soon to be the location for several theatres (and cinemas), the most famous being the Grand Opera House (see opposite), which opened in 1893 and later became the Dorchester cinema. Later, the Majestic was built on the site of a former Music Hall at the corner of Grimston Street (later known as the Criterion), and the Prince's Hall Cinema was built directly opposite the pub in 1910. The 1881 census listed Mr Bancroft alone at the pub, as a 70 year old beer-house keeper, and he remained as the licensee here until c.1890.

An 1891 sale notice in the Hull Advertiser gives what seems to be the only reference to the beer-house's name. Property belonging to Samuel Musgrave was auctioned, which included: 'the **Duke of Edinburgh** beer-house, 11 George Street, the shop at 12 George Street and two houses behind' [Norman's Court], which sold for a total of £1,700. David Bancroft retired c.1888 and one of his daughters (by then married) continued the licence. Sarah Elizabeth Rumley was listed as the beer-house keeper from 1889; the 1891 census shows that her widowed father continued to live there too. Sarah remained just a few years until her father's death in 1893. As a new tenant took over in 1894 the name was changed to the **Grand Hotel**, no doubt hoping to share the glory of the newly-built 'Grand Opera House' next-door-but-one. In the picture opposite, 11 is on the far right, then the entrance to Robinson's Court (originally Norman's Court), and then no.12. The next building, with a projecting ground floor, is no.13, which had been a Music Hall, and was later taken by Bentley's Brewery. This was originally

Sam Allon Collection

two shops with offices and rooms on the upper floors. Bentley's relocated in 1909, and these premises were used by the Hull Brewery Co from the 1920s until the 1950s. It appears that the licensed area of the Grand Hotel remained at 11 throughout, never expanding to take in the shop at 12, despite the large signboard at roof level stretching across the width of the whole building. Number 12 did become the Grand Recreation Club for a short time around 1924-25, and was managed by Harry Jones, who was licensee of the Grand pub at that time. The pub finally closed c.1927, and the owners Worthington's claimed £6,322 in compensation (but were actually paid £4,000 – £3,900 to the owners, and £100 to the licensee).

George Street was re-numbered from consecutive numbering, to the more common system of 'odds and evens' c.1931. To confuse things further, the new numbers also began from the opposite end of the street where it meets Savile Street, rather than Grimston Street where it had previously.

In 1902 the famous Carmichaels store had opened at 8 George Street, expanding to take in 9-10 next door to the Grand Hotel beer-house around 1919. The former pub premises had a variety of tenants until c.1960, at which time Carmichaels expanded again to take in the site of the old pub building within their store. Following Carmichaels closure in January 1991, the whole site was redeveloped as a long-standing club called Ven-U, which closed in 2013. The picture opposite dates from c.1908, top-left during demolition prior to Carmichaels c.1960 expansion, and top-right as the site appeared in September 2015.

Halfway Hotel, Hessle Road • In an 1855 directory Charles Fowler was listed as a 'porter merchant', Wold Ings, Hessle Road – shown as part of the 'Wold Ings Farm' on the 1852 Ordnance Survey plan. Charles was later listed as the victualler at the **Halfway House** in an 1858 trade directory (then within the parish of Swanland). The 1861 census lists 34 year-old Lincolnshire-born cattle dealer Isaac Houghton, with his wife, son, daughter and mother at the 'Half Way House, public house' on the High Road; Isaac Houghton had his ale-house licence renewed in August 1864, and is listed in the directories for the first time in 1863: 'Isaac Houghton, Halfway House, Hessle Road'. These early references to the Halfway pub relate to an older property than that we see today. It was always the contention of my late friend and mentor Graham Wilkinson that the old house shown to the left of the c.1960 picture above was the original Halfway Inn, with the present pub to its right. In the early 1870s the Halfway Inn was still out in the open fields as Hessle Road had not developed this far west, but as new streets were built off the main road and the frontage became built up, developers soon took interest in the old licensed premises. Having a current licence meant no new licence would have to be applied for. Consequently, in 1874, bricklayer James Richardson Wilford (brother of wines & spirit merchant Henry Wilford) acquired the licence of the Halfway and built a new property to its east, which is the building we see today; architect William Marshall designed the new building.[1] The style is very similar to the Criterion Hotel (page 119), and Marshall was also the architect of the Kingston Hotel, Trinity House Lane – all built in the ornate Gin Palace style of the day. Its original address had a similarly grand tone, being noted in the late 1870s as 'Edinburgh Crescent', Hessle Road. Hessle Road literally developed around the new **Halfway Hotel**, with new streets and properties being continually built in the

vicinity throughout the 1880s, following the boundary extension in 1882. James Wilford remained at the Halfway Hotel (by then numbered 474 Hessle Road, later 490) until 1900. Following a short tenure by George Beaumont, a member of a famous Hull family of publicans took charge of the Halfway. From c.1906 until the early 1920s Henry Rayner was proprietor before moving to the Star & Garter, Hessle Road (see page 167).

Despite the decline of the fishing industry, and the onslaught of demolition and redevelopment of the area, in true Hessle Road tradition the Halfway Hotel has kept on going, and continues to serve the locals of Newington to this day, as it has for at least 160 years. If you're ever out this way, stop and admire the beautiful decorative brickwork of this great survivor.

1. Hull History Centre, ref. OB Newington.11.

Holderness Hotel, Witham • Witham was formerly known as North Blockhouse Lane, and was renamed c.1780 after one of the larger landowners here, Mr Henry Witham of Nuttles Hall, Burstwick. No buildings are shown on the north-east side of Witham on plans of 1818, but by the time of Greenwood's 1835 plan of Hull, a small building is shown at the corner of Witham and Dansom Lane; an 1834 trade directory listed for the first time the **Holderness New Inn**, victualler John Wing.

This was a curious choice of name, as an older inn already existed further west along Witham, also called the Holderness New Inn. Despite this, both held the same name for many years. Several tenants came and went, and in October 1847 Thomas Wing acquired the pub. An advertisement he placed in the Hull Packet on 7 October 1847 noted:

'HOLDERNESS NEW INN,
CORNER OF DANSOM LANE, WITHAM.
THOS. WING (Driver of the Hornsea Mail)
begs to inform his Friends and the Public that he has taken and entered upon the above INN, and hopes to merit a share of Public Patronage. The Express London Daily Newspaper taken. Well-aired Beds, good Stabling and Lock-up Coach Houses.'

An 1848 trade directory noted Thomas Wing as a 'victualler & mail guard, Holderness New Inn, Dansom Lane'. The census of 1851 recorded 41 year-old Thomas as an 'inn keeper and post master employing two men'. With him at the inn were his wife, three sons, two daughters, and a servant. It appears he gave up the pub when the Hornsea coach was cancelled as plans were approved for the Hull to Hornsea railway line, on which work began in 1862. By 1863 Stephen Marshall had taken over the inn and it became known as

simply the **Holderness Inn** from that date – in an effort to end the confusion between the two identically named pubs. In 1869 the pub passed to Robert Marshall and became known as the **Holderness Hotel**. The name changes could have been linked to changes in brewer, as Bass took the pub when Marshall left, but the facts are hard to establish. However, in September 1897 an article in the Hull Daily Mail revealed that the two pubs were still apparently using the same name for licensing purposes:

'The Hull Licensing Justices were yesterday astonished to learn that there are two licensed houses in Witham, each known as the Holderness New Inn. As an application was made in respect to each house the cases got somewhat confused.'

From the beginning of the 20th century the name settled as Holderness Hotel, its address being firmly fixed as 55 Witham and 1 Dansom Lane. We have no clue to the appearance of the original inn, but it is likely that it was rebuilt or re-fronted later in the 19th century to appear as it does opposite in a photograph from 1904. However, we do know that it was re-fronted once more in 1914 in the mock-Tudor plaster and wood panelling, which required the loss of the ornate Victorian detailing illustrated opposite. From c.1926 the pub passed to Henry Wilson Ltd of Hull, reverting to Bass when they took over Wilson's. Local historian John Wilson Smith made a comprehensive survey of the 'Inns of Holderness' in the early 1950s, and noted when he visited the Holderness Hotel, that the old coach house was still in existence but converted to a beer cellar.

The photograph top-left dates from 1992 (after which the pub closed for a few years, reopening in 1999), and top-right from September 2015.

Hull History Centre

King Edward VII, Prospect Street • In 2015 there are no pubs in Prospect Street, but historically there have been at least four; the Cricketers Arms, the Hole in the Wall, the Wheatsheaf and King Edward VII.

In the 1791 trade directory for Hull, victualler Thomas *Linward* was listed at 'Beverley Gates' (the first development of buildings outside the old town gates at the end of Whitefriargate), and in an 1803 directory Thomas Linwood was listed at the **Blue Bell**, Prospect Street, almost certainly the same pub. By the 1831 trade directory the pub was listed as 3 Prospect Street. Stephenson's trade directory of 1842 noted that a victualler at the pub, Benjamin Wright, also ran livery stables that were situated in nearby Edward Street. At that time, a small court that was just north of the pub had become known as Blue Bell Yard, and is shown on the 1853 Ordnance Survey Plan. As seen in the 1920s photograph opposite, the buildings around the pub are clearly Georgian and the Blue Bell would originally have had a plain frontage, a door leading to a Bar with simple furnishings and a make-do counter over a barrel or two. Through a door to the rear was a separate room, which may have been either a Club-Room or a Smoking Room. The upstairs quarters may also have held a Club-Room and the living area of the victualler himself. It was common in these narrow houses to also have the kitchen upstairs. By 1875 the Blue Bell had become 6 Prospect Street, and re-named the **Prospect Inn**, presumably after Prospect Street.

When King Edward VII was proclaimed King in 1901, the Prospect Inn was re-named as the **King Edward VII Inn**, and a new street that was under construction nearby was hastily re-named King Edward Street. The old pub was redeveloped at that time, and the plain front replaced in the more elaborate Edwardian style of the day. The first and second storey windows were made into opposing curved and square bays, and projected to suggest a jettied frontage. In a curiously contradictory way the roof was fronted with a projecting pedimented gable suggesting a neo-classical style, possibly a detail carried over from the last style period. On the ground floor a ceramic tile frontage was added (probably in green) and the upper storeys were stuccoed with ornate plaster detailing, reminiscent of other pubs of the period (e.g. the Empress Hotel, Alfred Gelder Street). In May 1941, at the height of the Second World War, the whole of this section of Prospect Street was badly damaged following direct hits during an overnight blitz. The photograph above shows the remains of the pub being bulldozed to the ground. A new King Edward VII pub opened in Anlaby Road, on the corner of Anne Street, in October 1957.

The site of the shops and the old pub was cleared, and the old street line brought forward and levelled, and in February 1956 a new Woolworths store was opened taking in the site of the pub. Woolworths closed several years ago and their old shop is currently used by Bargain Buys.

Kingston Hotel, Cumberland Street • Tucked away in the middle of industrial Sculcoates is a real survivor of a pub. Despite the gradual loss of all of the housing in the area the **Kingston Hotel** continues to trade in 2015. It was in September 1846 that the Brewster (licensing) Sessions first recorded a licence being approved for the pub:

> 'Mr. Sidebottom, on behalf of Mr Rayment of the Kingston-hotel, near the Kingston Cotton-mills, who applied at the last sitting of the magistrates for a licence and was refused, attending before the court with an improved plan of the premises ... Mr. Ayre, said he accompanied the Mayor to examine the premises in question, when the Mayor expressed his opinion that a public-house would be required in the neighbourhood, but thought Rayment's too small. The [new] plan certainly presented the premises to be more extensive than the bench anticipated.'

The new pub was one of three within a few doors of each other, including the Kingston Arms, and the Gardeners Arms, also trading c.1851. Back at the Kingston Hotel, William Rayment was keen to profit from the influx of workers that was required to serve the Kingston Cotton Mill complex across the road. Established in 1845, the buildings and chimneys of the mill dominated the area for more than a century. The 1851 census records William as a 41 year-old innkeeper, with his wife, niece and one lodger. The Rayment family remained at the Kingston Hotel until c.1870, despite the death of William in 1863. His wife 'Anne' (actually Angelina) was the last in the family to hold the Kingston's licence; Angelina died in 1868 aged just 50. The Kingston held a singing & music licence, meaning that not only could music he played or made on the premises, but that the visitors to the pub were also legally allowed to sing along. In the late 19th century the Kingston was home to the Hull Britannia football club, and the East Sculcoates Music Society, hosting numerous sporting dinners and meetings. The frontage we see today is from a 1924 reconstruction, which included the addition of the mansard roof, and minor internal changes.[2] Shown on the opposite page c.1926, and left in the 1960s, with an 1855 advertisement below.

W. RAYMENT,
KINGSTON HOTEL,
OPPOSITE THE KINGSTON COTTON MILLS,
CUMBERLAND-STREET, SCULCOATES,
HULL.

Excellent Wines, Spirits, Ale, Porter, Cigars, &c.
GOOD AND WELL AIRED BEDS.
A Fine Collection of Birds, Animals, &c.—Admission Free.

2. Hull History Centre, ref. 1916M.2604 (completed 13 November 1924).

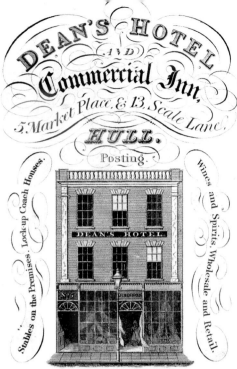

John Wyles

In a city called Kingston upon Hull it is no surprise that the Kingston Hotel in Cumberland Street, shown on the previous pages, was not the only pub to feature the word 'Kingston' in its name. There was also the **Kingston Hotel**, at 5 Market Place & 13 Scale Lane shown above-centre in an advertisement from the 1840s when in the hands of Frances & Henry Dean. Deeds for the building date from before 1752, and it began life as a Coffee House latterly known as the Dog & Duck, before changing its name to the Kingston Hotel c.1830. A corner property, it also included 13 Scale Lane, where for many years a separate licensed property was situated known as the **Kingston Hotel Tap**. The pubs were was demolished c.1874, when the site was appropriated for a new Post Office.

Shown opposite c.1910 is the grand **Kingston Hotel**, at the corner of Trinity House Lane and North Church Side, originally known as the **Windmill Inn**, which had stood here since the beginning of the 18th century. Noted in the directories from c.1810, the old pub was rebuilt in 1877 when the licensing judges heard the owner Edward Coney's plea for a licence extension:

'Edward Coney, of the Windmill Inn, Trinty House-lane, applied for an extension of his licence to premises which have been rebuilt. A dwelling-house, a piece of vacant ground near the corner of Trinity House-lane and North Church-side, and two shops or dwelling-houses on North Church-side, all adjoining, have been taken in'.

Dr Rollit, who appeared in support, said that a very handsome hotel had been built, but the judges voiced their disapproval at such a large pub being built opposite: 'one of the finest edifices in England' [Holy Trinity]. The Kingston continues to trade in 2015, and remains one of Hull's most beautiful pub buildings.

Top-left is the **Kingston Arms**, at the corner of Thomas Street and Strawberry Street, which first opened c.1850, as the streets were just being laid-out amidst vast strawberry gardens south of the Holderness Road. Charles Lowery was the first named victualler at the 'Kingston Arms Inn' in a trade directory of 1851. Shown above-left in the 1950s, the still popular little pub continues to trade in 2015 (see image bottom-left on page 115).

The only other pub in Hull that made use of the word 'Kingston' was the **Kingston New Inn** at 6 Hopwood Street, near the corner of Freehold Street. The first mention of the pub is in a newspaper article in December 1854, when an inquest was held here regarding an accidental death. The first licensee was William Woodrough who sold the property in 1856 and the licence ceased. Despite several requests for a 'new' licence for the pub from 1860, it was not until August 1864 that one was granted again, when the licence of the Whale Fishery in Wilmington was transferred here. The pub is shown above-right in a photograph made just prior to the demolition of the buildings in the street in the 1980s, the pub having closed c.1974.

Lion Inn, Francis Street • Francis Street (east) was laid out in 1822 on land belonging to George Pryme MP, and named after his grandfather, who had been mayor of Hull in 1749 and 1766, as well as sheriff of Hull in 1745. The new street formed the basis of a typically greedy development of terraced houses, with shamelessly poorly-built courts behind, all crowded onto small inadequate plots with drainage so poor that it was still being complained about in the press in the 1840s. The same development later included Christopher Street (after Christopher Pryme), Alicia Street (Alicia was Pryme's daughter), and Reform Street (in honour of the reformed House of Commons to which Pryme had been elected). As has previously been explained, the proposed pubs in new developments were often built first and used as site offices; the building shown here, at the corner of Francis Street and Christopher Street, was constructed c.1825-30.

Cabinet maker George Young (late of 6 Dock Office Row) was the first recorded occupant c.1835. He was listed as a beer retailer at 35 Francis Street in a trade directory that year. An 1838 directory noted: 'George Young, cabinet maker & beer-house keeper, corner of Francis Street and Christopher Street'. The 1841 census recorded George, aged 35, still with cabinet maker as his main occupation, with his wife and five children. By 1851 George was listed as an 'organ builder' at his 'beer-house', by then re-numbered as 30 Francis Street. It was not until an 1863 directory that the pub was mentioned by name, when Mr Robert Beecroft was noted as a beer-seller at the **Lion Tavern**, Francis Street East. Occasionally recorded as the **Red Lion** in the 1870s, the pub name settled as the **Lion Inn** from the late 1870s and its address was fixed as 28-30 Francis Street East. During the 1880s the compact pub was home to the Duke of Edinburgh Lodge of the United Order of Freemasons Friendly Society.

Almost all of the property in this area was systematically cleared under compulsory purchase, which started in the late 1930s and ended with the widespread and ill-judged clearance in preparation for Freetown Way in the 1980s. The Lion Inn, and its neighbour across the street, the Seedcrushers Arms, stood isolated from c.1938, as it had when first built over a century earlier. Following closure in 1949 its licence was transferred to the Kingston Hotel, Trinity House Lane and the Lion was finally demolished in the early 1950s to make way for the construction of the Clover Dairies warehouse and factory which remains today under new owners.

The picture opposite dates from c.1910, top-right from c.1926, and top-left from c.1950, just as the pub was about to be demolished.

London Hotel, Queen Street • An 1819 news report mentions: 'the house of William Senior known by the name of the **London Tavern**'. This is the earliest mention of the huge premises shown opposite in a photograph from c.1910. William Senior remained here until c.1831 by which time it was also the offices of the London steam packet. James Glover, who took over the business c.1831, made the 'extensively enlarged' premises famous as **Glover's London Hotel**. It was so well-known locally that when William Morrison took over c.1874 he continued to mention the previous owner's name in his advertising (see above-right). Situated in Queen Street, at the corner with Humber Street, the London Hotel also had a 'tap' entered from Humber Street, which was listed separately from the hotel for many years.

In the late 1830s and 1840s William Roberts was listed as the 'tap keeper', in Humber Street, his home address initially being 2 Leek's Entry – also nearby in Humber Street. He was also coachman at the hotel. Enjoying good trade from the ferry, steamers and the fruit market, the pub thrived until the Second World War, when it was closed on 8 May 1941 following blitz damage. In 1996 a pub called **The Heritage** was built on part of the footprint of the London Hotel, known as **Ruscadors** from 2008, but it too closed in 2014. That building was demolished for a new development called C4Di, which stretches east across the historic site of the Georgian South End Graving Dock (dating from the 1780s), the South End Battery of the Hull Garrison, and to the south over the site of the South End Brewery, to name but a few.

Wilberforce House · Hull Museums

Manchester Arms, Scale Lane • One of the Old Town's longest-standing licensed premises, the view from the window of the Manchester Arms in Scale Lane has changed considerably in its 200-plus years history as a pub. Although perhaps not quite as old as its adjoining neighbour – 'the oldest house in Hull' – the original building was perhaps of the 17th century. Although it may have been a pub earlier, it was not until 1810 that the **Blade Bone** was first recorded, the victualler being Thomas Shepherdson. The premises, listed as 6 Scale Lane had several changes of name, being the re-interpreted **Splaw Bone** (1831), **Earl Grey** (1834), and the **Black Bull Inn** from c.1838. In 1874 the pub transferred to Thomas Foston who retained the name until 1876 when he changed it to the **Manchester Arms**. Throughout the changes of name, the recorded number of the pub also varied from 6 to 7 Scale Lane and back again.

Shown above-right is a drawing by the artist F S Smith showing Scale Lane in 1883 looking west towards the junction with Lowgate and Silver Street. On the immediate left is 5 Scale Lane, and adjoining it is the Manchester Arms. Note that this was the original building, which, like its equally ancient neighbours, was much nearer to the roadway. On the right of 5, and the left

of 6 (the pub) are the entrances to two passages that ran parallel and gave separate access to the yards of each property. In March 1887 a new landlord Tom Spence placed an advert in the Hull Daily Mail noting:

> 'MANCHESTER ARMS, SCALE LANE --------
> Opened under New Management, after extensive alterations, with a choice of Wines and Spirits. The best ales in Hull at 2d. per pint.'

It was in September 1896 that local architects Smith, Brodrick & Lowther drew plans for the major reconstruction of the Manchester Arms.[3] It was at this point that the pub was set back from the road, with a six foot portion of land at the front sold to the Hull Corporation. Shown opposite c.1926, the door on the left led via a passage to a 'bottle & jug' area, separated from the bar with a screen. The present layout is much-changed from that of 1896. The continuing and very welcome resurgence of the pub scene in the Scale Lane area harks back to the 19th century, when in Scale Lane alone there were at least eight pubs. Even the oldest house in Hull next door to the Manchester Arms is a Bistro & Craft Beer bar these days, known as The Old House since c.2013.

3. Hull History Centre, ref. 1894M.1098.

Frank Farnsworth Collection

Minerva Hotel, Nelson Street • An article in the Hull Packet newspaper of 7 October 1828 noted that during the annual Brewster Sessions:

> 'The only new licence, for many years, was granted on this occasion to Mr. Richd. Cortis, formerly Master of the London steam-packet, for a house at the corner of Minerva Terrace, which is to be called the Minerva Hotel. The number of publicans in this town is 226.'

Thus the **Minerva Hotel** opened in 1828, and Richard Cortis was listed in the trade directories at the Minerva until c.1852. Initially numbered 5 Minerva Terrace, in 1831 Cortis announced to the public that he had: 'added the adjoining house to his establishment'. Where 4 Minerva Terrace was added can be seen clearly as a raised break in the brick frontage running the height of the building. At this point the hotel's original symmetrical appearance was lost. During the late 1830s the numbering of Minerva Terrace was reversed, the hotel becoming 1 & 2, rather than 4 & 5. At that time, c.1838, a smaller licensed building was added as a 'tap' to the hotel; this obscured the large lettering spelling out 'CORTIS' on the gable wall, which was not revealed again until 1985 when the tap was demolished (see top-right). Joseph Day was the 'tap-keeper', first recorded there from 1839. The 'Minerva Wines & Spirits Vaults' (the tap) can be seen in the c.1900 photograph opposite; note the original cast-iron urinal – the precursor of today's brick-built structure. From c.1906 the Minerva was re-numbered once more as 15-17 Nelson Street.

The Minerva was extensively refurbished internally in 1984-85, at which point the old vaults were also lost (my photo bottom-right is from c.1983), but in their place a small brew-house was constructed that remains to this day. The Minerva 'brewpub' was the fourth to be opened by Tetley's, and continued brewing until the late 1990s.

Note the old Stevens & Sons confectionery shop, also visible in the 1980s photograph top-right, the frontage of which was saved and rebuilt in the Street Life Museum.

John Wyles

Newington Hotel, Anlaby Road • In August 1861 the Hull Packet newspaper ran an advertisement for the sale of various building materials at 'Mr Easton's yard, near the **Wold Carr Inn**'. This appears to be the first reference to the pub that stands on the corner of Anlaby Road and Walton Street. The 1861 census confirmed James Mitchell's tenancy at the pub, when he was listed as an inn keeper there, aged 35, with his wife, son and mother. At that time the pub was adjacent to a turn-pike toll-bar gate, as the Anlaby Road was at that time still only passable at certain points by payment of a fee (the gate was removed in c.1874 as the turnpikes were abolished).

A change in owner in 1867 brought a new name for the pub when it transferred to Samuel Butler Whittaker, who changed the name to the **Newington Hotel** by 1873. It is very likely that the original Wold Carr Inn was a smaller building than that we see today, and it seems too coincidental that the terrace built opposite (Cumberland Terrace) that also dated from c.1872-73, matched the Newington Hotel symmetrically, suggesting they were built together. The two can be compared in the 1920s photograph middle-right opposite. Originally of three storeys, the pub's top third was removed following blitz damage during the Second World War bombings.

Widow Mrs Stella M Lamplugh was noted here from 1900, and in 1901 she married Ernest Parker. Her name S M Parker can be seen on the sign-board in the c.1908 photograph on the opposite page, and the name PARKER'S above the corner door. Husband Ernest Parker held the licence from c.1908 and remained until 1936. In 1909 the pub had a new farriers shop, bottle store and shed built for a total cost of £195. The Parker family became well-known and the pub was referred to locally as Parker's from the outset. Much later, during the 1980s, the name of the pub was officially changed to **Parker's**.

Clearly visible in the 1920s photograph centre-right is a large stone 'M&R' at the corner, stretching the full height of the ground floor. This was added by the owners Moors' & Robson's Brewery during a major refurbishment in the 1920s, replacing the original corner door. It was during this refurbishment that the exterior details shown on the photograph opposite were also lost. The building was extended along its Anlaby Road frontage to take in the former shop next door, in the occupation of a confectioner-barber-tobacconist at the time of the photo. A single storey addition was also created along the Walton Street elevation, visible in both photographs right.

The stylish Art-Deco monogram was also later removed (or covered) – perhaps when Moors' & Robson's were taken over by Hewitt Brothers of Grimsby in 1960 – leaving the blank panel we see today. In 2014 the pub was renamed as **The Boot Room**, and the last traces of the old Newington pub were lost.

Oak Vaults, Scott Street • In 1830 William Peacock opened a new beer-house in Scott Street, which may have been the origins of the pub shown here. By 1834, James Binks is listed as a beer retailer at 35 Scott Street, and in a later 1838 directory he is named as a joiner at the **Royal Oak Inn**, 35 Scott Street, at the corner of Lockwood Street.

Around the turn of the 20th century the pub was also known as the **Royal Oak Recreation Club** and hosted several local sports teams and their many meetings, dinners and celebrations, including the wonderfully named Oak Vaults Tourist Club, which appears to have been a domino team.

Shown opposite in the late 1920s, the name board on the pub shows it had long-been known as **Oak Vaults**, but continued to be listed in directories as the Royal Oak Inn until after the Second World War.

In 1934 the pub was refurbished internally, and externally was altered to the frontage we see today by Moors' & Robson's Brewery. The traditional Victorian exterior was replaced in 1935 with a with 'rustic-brick' detailing, surrounding repeated 'M&R' logos cut into stone panels. The simple sign board was replaced by a finely lettered Art Deco stone plaque stretching along the Scott Street frontage that confirmed 'OAK VAULTS'. The architect was Frederick Robson of the brewery.[4] This was another pub where a half-hearted effort was made to remove any trace of the former brewery,

probably when Moors' & Robson's were taken over by Hewitts in 1960; the four sets of M&R initials were filled with render, which only served to make them stand out even more.

Situated in an area where all pubs struggle to earn their upkeep, after a period of sporadic opening the Oak Vaults finally closed in 2009. It was advertised for sale as a 'five-bedroom detached house' in 2011, and in 2012 a planning application was submitted for 'change of use from public house to mixed use of public house and health spa'. At the time of writing the building remains closed, and despite some unfortunate changes, the owners have at least accentuated the surviving 1930s Moors' & Robson's details, bringing back to life the M&R and OAK VAULTS lettering.

Just visible on the far-left of the old photograph is another 'lost pub' the **Hull & Barnsley Arms**, which opened around the same time as the Royal Oak Inn, and was first named the **Rob Roy Inn**. The date at which it became known as the Hull & Barnsley Arms is unclear, but it was between 1888, when plans were submitted for alterations to the Rob Roy Inn, and 1895 when the tenant of the Hull & Barnsley Arms sought new staff in a newspaper. It closed in 1960 but the original building still exists in-part beneath modern exterior cladding.

Hull History Centre

4. Hull History Centre, ref. 1929M.3210 (approved in February 1935).

Queen's Hotel, Charlotte Street • In August 1875, almost a century after the property here was constructed, solicitor Mr Spink appeared at the annual Hull Brewster Sessions (held in the Town Hall), on behalf of Henry White of the **Queen's Hotel**, Charlotte Street for a licence for a commercial hotel:

> 'Mr White did not wish to occupy the premises as spirit vaults or a dram-shop, and applied for an hotel licence merely. As the magistrates were aware, the premises were opened in February last, and his client now came to ask them to enable him to supply his visitors with their requirements.'

The building had formerly been used as a private school run by James Bird, at 15 Charlotte Street, at the corner of Charlotte Street Mews. The 1871 census records James, his wife, four sons, two daughters, seven staff and 16 pupils resident at this one address. Although the address was given as Charlotte Street, it's clear from the c.1926 photograph on the opposite page that the original entrance was in Charlotte Street Mews. The smaller image (left) shows the location in 1905, with the Alexandra Theatre visible far right. Redevelopment took place at the pub in 1934, to the designs of Wellsted, Dossor & Wellsted, when the whole appearance of the building changed and doors were inserted in the George Street elevation.[5] It was re-numbered 141 George Street following the rebuilding of the North Bridge in 1931, when the road alignment here was altered. In 1961 the property next door was also taken by the owner Hull Brewery and opened as the Queen's Restaurant, designed by the Hull architect D Priestman[6], as seen in the 1960s photo above. Closing in 1999, the pub and restaurant was converted to a club in 2000 called **Reflections**, which more recently (c.2007) became the very popular **Pozition** nightclub, which has extended even further west along the street.

5. Hull History Centre, ref. 1926M.1137.
6. Ibid. ref. 1953M.9685.

Royal Oak, Prince's Dock Side • Originally licenced in the 1750s, this pub almost certainly started life as a single-storey dwelling, possibly forming part of the original town walls within the entrance known as the Postern Gate. Richard Oliver was the first victualler to be named in trade directories, in 1791. The pub's original address was therefore Posterngate, but following the construction of Humber Dock to the south (now the Marina), a street was laid out around 1810 linking the top of Whitefriargate to the Humber Dock Side; this was called New Dock Street. It's hard to imagine now, but as the new street developed (built on the site of the old town ramparts) it had houses on both sides. In preparation for another new dock called Junction Dock, which linked the older Queen's Dock (now Queen's Gardens) and Humber Dock, the street was renamed Junction Dock Street during the late 1830s. It then became Prince's Dock Side when the dock was re-named. The pub continued to be known as **The Royal Oak** throughout.

Evidence of the pub's Posterngate address is the placement of a door there, which is visible in the 1930s photograph on the opposite page, that was later altered to become a window. By c.1842 the pub's address had become fixed as 22 Junction Dock Street, and it is likely that the present frontage dates from that period, with surprisingly little alteration.

From the late 1990s it was known as **Quayside**, with an increasing shift towards food. The Quayside changed name around 2009, becoming **Leonardo's@ Quayside**, the new owners telling the press that: 'it is still a pub, but probably a bistro-pub'. Leonardo's hadn't moved far – just across the road from Prince's Quay, where it had been a popular Italian restaurant since the shopping centre opened. The image bottom-left dates from c.1972, and bottom-right is a photo of the short-lived enclosed beer-garden in Posterngate. This was known as **Royal Oak Garden** in the 1980s.

St Leger Hotel, Paragon Street • An advertisement appeared in the Hull Advertiser on 10 July 1802, which read:

> 'TO CONTRACTORS, FOR MAKING OF STREETS, DRAINS, FLAGGING OF STREETS, &c.
>
> A STREET is intended to be made, called PARAGON STREET, to commence at Waterworks Street, and continue in a direct line through Portas's Garden, about 620 feet long, and 45 feet broad.'

Thus Paragon Street was laid out, but building work was sporadic and by the 1840s several plots remained unbuilt. Although not shown on Stephenson's plan of Hull in 1842, by September 1844 'newly-built' dwelling houses were being sold in the newly created Little Queen Street. By the time Wilkinson's plan of Hull was published in 1848, a property was shown on the south-west corner of Little Queen Street. The street itself had been laid out in or around 1837, and 'flagged and paved' in 1845. The area was developed by builder John Siminson, who had purchased this and other land in the area from Henry Broadley in 1841 (Broadley's diaries for that year record letters from Siminson in January about the subject). Siminson named a gallery in Little Queen Street after himself as record of his ownership.

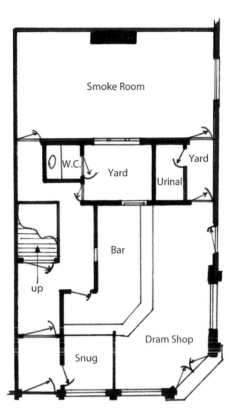

In a trade directory of 1846 the corner property was listed as the premises of plumber William Appleyard, who remained until at least 1861. In 1863 it was listed as a beer-house for probably the first time. **The Druids Arms**, 8 Paragon Street, was kept by John Ward, and became the fifth drinking establishment on the north side of the street alone. Druids Arms was most likely a reference to one of the friendly societies who may have met there. By 1888 the pub was kept by William Williams and renamed around 1892 as the **St. Leger Hotel**. The St. Leger was a popular horse race and was most likely the inspiration for the naming of the pub.

In 1901 the St. Leger was tied to Moors' & Robson's Brewery for the first time, and plans drawn in 1907 by Habron & Robson of Spring Bank, gave an idea of the layout at the time (shown above, re-drawn from DPM.30.126 Hull History Centre). The plans, drawn up for proposed alterations, show the pub as it was, with a corner door leading into an L-shaped dram shop. The dram shop shared a counter with a tiny snug, accessible from a separate entrance further along Paragon Street and visible in the c.1910 photograph opposite. When entering from Paragon Street, if you were to carry on past the snug entrance and follow the passage to the rear of the buildings, you would find yourself in the largest of the St. Leger's rooms; the smoke room, 22 feet by 11, had been created from the shell of a former private house at 1 Little Queen Street. On the first floor was a small club-room similar to many of the other beer-houses in the area, and this would have been the room used by the friendly society mentioned earlier (possibly the United Ancient Order of Druids, which had opened in Hull for the first time in 1838). Another victim of the stiff competition in the area, the St. Leger was referred to the compensation committee several times by the Police and was subsequently made redundant in 1923. The owners claimed £6,038-16s-4d but received only £5,000. It was then sold at auction for £3,100 in 1925, and was reopened – still as the St. Leger – by Frank Bricklebank who kept it until closure c.1930. Later it was taken in by the extended White House property next door, and formed part of a wine bar named **Scribes**, attached to the Berni Inn. This remained into the 1990s, and also had an entrance from Jameson Street at the rear. From c.1994 until 2008 the Paragon Street property was a **Yates Wine Lodge**, and then the **Kingston Tavern**, a very short-lived pub that closed within a year, and the property has remained empty ever since.

Stag Inn, Leonard Street • Leonard Street initially stretched from Beverley Road all the way to Peel Street, as one long street. The 1861 census recorded William Botham, a 25 year-old grocer at 20 Leonard Street, and next door at 19 was John Craven, a 52 year-old butcher and gardener. Both properties were situated on the south side of the street, near to the entrance of Beaulah Place, a short terrace of small houses.

Leonard Street was still being built upon at that time, and the section between Walmsley Street and Freehold Street had several gaps inbetween properties. In 1862 builder Richard Wilkins of Norfolk Street had plans approved for three adjoining houses in Leonard Street, and two others adjacent in Beaulah Place. Number 16 was a confectioner's shop and 14 & 15 were named as a new beer-house.[8]

By July 1862 both Craven and Botham were listed as beer-retailers in Leonard Street, and in a news report in that month when...

> 'John Craven and Wm Botham, beer-house keepers, Leonard-street, were each fined 10s and costs for selling beer after eleven o'clock on Saturday night.'

The 1871 census listed Thomas Holmes as a publican and commercial traveller at the pub (14 Leonard Street), named in the census as the **Stag Inn**. Around 1881 George Johnson took over the Stag Inn, remaining until 1915. In August 1896 George advertised for staff:

> 'WANTED, a good, clean General, for a family of two, to occasionally assist in bar; washing put out; wages from £16 to £20. — Stag Inn, Leonard Street.'

It is during George's tenancy that the pub is shown opposite, in a photograph that was reproduced as a publicity postcard c.1908. No doubt that is George and his wife Rachel posing for the photographer. Upon his retirement in 1915 George was honoured with several dinners, having been at one time a master baker at the Hull Workhouse, a well-known sportsman, and one of the founders of the Hull & District Beer, Spirit and Wine Trade Association; he was presented with a silver-handled umbrella and a cheque. The Stag Inn was, somewhat unusually, owned by brewers Warwick & Richardson of Newark on Trent, and remained so until at least the 1950s. The popular little back-street pub remained open until 1976, but was demolished in the 1980s. At that time, new housing was built in the area and the once long Leonard Street was foreshortened. Its entrance remains at the Beverley Road (east) end, but the section that once included the Stag Inn is now built upon and a footpath links through to the now disconnected (west) end of the street. The site of the pub and Beulah Place are marked by typical 1980s council housing.

The derelict former Stag Inn is shown bottom-left just prior to demolition.

John Wyles

7. Hull History Centre, ref. OB.1328.

STAR AND GARTER.

STAR & GARTER

Star & Garter, Hessle Road • In August 1875 a licence was applied for a: 'public house to be called **Heron's Hotel**, now in the course of erection on the Hessle Road, near the site of the old toll bar, to be kept by Mr. Henry Heron'. Henry Heron was a former stonemason who had yards in Osborne Street, and a residence at 2 Villa Place in the late 1850s. A drama unfolded just a few years after the pub was built, when in November 1877:

> 'The large new building, known as Heron's Hotel, on the Hessle-road, opposite the cemetery, has been completely destroyed by fire. At 11.15 last Friday night, when Mr. Heron and his family retired to rest, everything appeared to be safe. The fire was discovered at two o'clock. A messenger was sent for the Newington fire-engine, which is kept at the Water-works, but for some unexplained cause no engine arrived at the fire. A second messenger was despatched to the Parliament-street police-station, and Inspector Dodsworth at once proceeded with the hose and a body of police to the scene of the fire. In the meantime nothing could be done to stay the ravages of the flames, and owing to the fact that a large amount of wood had been used in constructing the hotel, and there being a steady wind blowing, the fire spread rapidly. It was after four o'clock before water was thrown on to the building. It is surmised that it originated in the kitchen.'

Fortunately the family survived, and as most of the property was insured, in January 1878 plans were drawn up for: 'rebuilding Heron's Hotel – corner of Dock Avenue and Hessle Road', for Henry Heron. The newly built property used a lot of very substantial stone on the exterior, possibly in a reaction to the earlier fire, and the impressive new pub building was soon sold at auction. In 1879 George Cartwright was the first landlord of the re-built pub, re-named the **Star & Garter**, and on the exact site of Heron's Hotel. Mr Cartwright remained until 1908, and his wife Frances continued the licence until 1912. By then numbered as 325 Hessle Road, the Star & Garter Hotel took its place as one of the many Hessle Road pubs used by dock workers, fishermen and the 'weekend millionaires' fresh from the trawlers, establishing the close-knit drinking community that remains today.

From c.1924 Henry Rayner was landlord, from a famous local family that had held at least 10 pubs around the city since the early 1800s. Henry was late of the Halfway Hotel, mentioned earlier in this chapter. Since c.1990 the Star & Garter has used the name of that famous family as its own, and has become officially known as **Rayner's**.

The pub is shown opposite c.1926 with a 1920s advertisement, and below-right in the 1960s; note the bunches of grapes, in stone, that form the keystones of the first-floor window arches, above the unique and relatively unchanged frontage.

Strickland Arms, Strickland Street • Strickland Street was laid out off the south side of Hessle Road in 1872, one of the many streets built along the new road during the housing boom of that period. On the east side of the new street was a purpose-built beer-house, situated at 29 Strickland Street, at the corner of the unusually named Sagan Terrace. Strickland Street was at that time still in open fields with wide views across the Humber.

An application was first made for a beer & wine licence for the new pub in August 1873, but refused. The following August a beer-house licence was approved for Thomas Mallinson Stirk for the **Strickland Arms**, Strickland Street. In 1874 an application for a full ale-house licence was refused, and a spirit licence also refused in 1875, when the Hull Advertiser reported:

'Dr. Rollit, on behalf of Thomas Mallinson Stirk, made application for a spirit licence for the Strickland Arms, Strickland Street. The house was the resort of a large number of the fishing population of the town, and Mr. Stirk built these premises on the understanding with his customers that he should apply for a spirit licence, and, therefore, if he did not get his application granted he would be a martyr to his own philanthropy and good nature. The neighbourhood was extremely populous; there were fully 1,000 new houses, and the whole of them tenanted.

Opposed by Messrs Gibson Brothers, owners of property in the area, and on behalf of a number of fisherman who were against the application.

During the 1880s the pub was a popular resort of the local Conservatives, and meetings of the Coltman Ward Conservative Association were frequently held here. In the 1890s it had its own Strickland Arms Recreation Club, which had many trips end events, and was by then owned by T Linsley & Co, of Mytongate. Following the loss of custom from the declining fishing industry, and the demolition of the housing in the area during the 1960s and 1970s, the Strickland Arms struggled to remain open.

Like so many pubs in what has become an almost completely industrial area, it has closed and re-opened several times but managed to mostly remain open throughout.

When re-opening again in 2000, the pub was featured in an article in the Hull Daily Mail entitled: 'Customers can surf the net in Hull's first cyber-pub'. Even this attraction wasn't enough to keep the pub open and it closed once more. In 2011 it was re-opened again as a free house known as the Stricky' Arms, one of very few pubs in Hull that served Samuel Smith's Tadcaster ales. In 2015 things appear very quiet again in Strickland Street.

Wilberforce House • Hull Museums

Tally Ho Hotel, Bond Street • The original pub on this site dated from the late 18th century, and that building can be seen in the sketch shown above, that was drawn by the artist Frederick Schultz Smith in 1889. The pub was mentioned in 1805, when John Welbrock acquired Mrs E. Eggleston's, Fox Street Brewery and the **Tally Ho Inn**, Bond Street. During the 1830s landlord James Lloyd was also a mail guard on the mail coach. A Hackney Carriage Licence was repeatedly issued to another landlord, Henry Remington Guy, in the 1830s, who was also noted as a coach & cab proprietor throughout the 1840s and into the 1850s. In the 1860s the pub was also known as the **Sing Tally Ho!** – the landlord Arthur Cornell being a shoeing smith, with premises in nearby Wells Yard.
The pub was tied to Moors' & Robson's in 1895, and shortly after the site was required for street improvements to the city centre that culminated in the construction of the first section of Jameson Street. Previously there had been a warren of narrow alleys and streets here, which were mostly unsanitary, and did not suit the new traffic levels – especially the new trams. The owner and licensee were left with little choice in the matter, as in September 1901 it was reported that the corporation had: 'acquired a small strip of land right across the entire frontage for the widening of Bond Street'. Consequently, the old pub was rebuilt very near to its original site in 1902, the work carried out by G Scott at a cost of £2,043. The Tally Ho was again compulsory purchased in 1954, closing in 1957, along with the King William IV that stood almost opposite at the dog-leg end of Bond Street. Both pubs fell within an area that was demolished for further street improvements, and their licences then transferred to the new Viking pub on Shannon Road in 1960. The large former Co-op building was built on the site, and Bond Street realigned as a straight dual-carriageway.
Opposite is the newly rebuilt pub c.1905, with the Davis Street entrance visible on the far-right, and Jameson Street in the background. Centre-right is a card issued by the proprietor after the re-building. Bottom-right is the interior of the new pub with landlord Tommy Bilham, a well-known championship wrestler, weight-lifter and local celebrity, who held the pub from the 1930s to the 1950s.

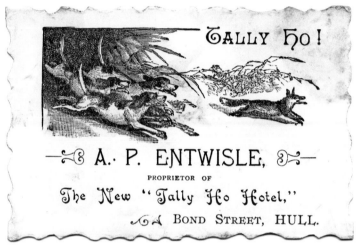

Private collection

Vauxhall Tavern, Hessle Road • Cragg's 1817 plan of Hull shows buildings on this site, at the corner of what was then Patrick Ground Lane (now Hessle Road) and Cent Per Cent Street (now St James Street). At the time of the plan the area remained mostly made up of gardens, for the supply of fruit and vegetables to the expanding town of Hull, and increasingly – for pleasure. It was not unusual for the refreshment facilities in these gardens to become licensed premises when well-established. A pub known as the **Stewart's Inn** (after wine merchant Charles Stewart) stood on this site, and was noted for sale in the press in 1813. John Myers was named as the occupant and its address was given as the north end of Cent-Per-Cent Street, in Patrick Ground Lane. The inn was also recorded in directories from 1817-1823, with its address still given as Patrick Ground Lane.

The building we see today is almost certainly the original Stewart's Inn, but records are inconclusive. The architectural details such as the shallow bow windows, are exactly the same as other buildings of the period, for example those as the corner of Grimston Street and Jarratt Street, which date from c.1810. The architectural evidence strongly suggests the present Vauxhall Tavern dates from c.1810-1815.

It was not until 1825-26 that it was named as the **Vauxhall Tavern** in the directories, Robert Johnson the first named landlord. In July that year the 'Hessle New Road' was first opened, and the pub became no.1 Hessle Road, which it remains to this day. In London at this time the Vauxhall Pleasure Gardens were very popular and perhaps the pub's close proximity to similar pleasure gardens may have inspired the name. Hull's 'Vauxhall Tea Gardens' remained in use until the 1840s. Whilst the upper floors of the pub remain relatively unchanged, sadly the ground floor has seen many alterations. The earliest image that I have found is the drawing made by the artist F S Smith in 1891 shown

above; note the panelling below the ground floor windows. By the time of the c.1926 photograph opposite the panelling had been replaced with the present granite, and the windows changed. The 1960s photograph above reveals more changes, including the loss of the fine Victorian details on the ground floor, and the removal of the shop frontage on the St James Street elevation. The granite lower ground floor frontage may have prevented further damage when the pub was one of the victims of the Humber tidal surge in 2013, which required a £50,000 re-fit. The pub has been known as **Frankie's Vauxhall Tavern** for many years, after a previous owner of the pub, and remains an extremely popular venue.

Bibliography & Thanks

P. Aldabella & R. Barnard. Hull and East Yorkshire Breweries, East Yorkshire Local History Society booklet no.50. Hull, 1997.

K. J. Allison (editor). Victoria County History of the County of York and the East Riding. Volume 1. The City of Kingston upon Hull, Oxford University Press for the Institute of Historical Research. 1969.

Anon. Yorkshire by Pen and Picture, A. Brown & Sons. Hull, 1915.

R. Barnard. Ale & Architecture, Four Old Town Pubs, Hull College Local History Unit. Hull, 1996.

R. Barnard. High Street, Hull (1673-1798) Work in Progress, Hull College Local History Unit. Hull, 2002.

R Barnard. Moors' & Robson's Breweries Ltd, A Brief History, Hull College Local History Unit. Hull, 1996.

R. Curry. Last Complete Performance: In Memory of Hull's Cinemas, Hutton Press and Hull College Local History Unit. Cherry Burton, 1992.

T. Dodsworth. Hull & East Riding Early Days on the Road; A Photographic Record, Hutton Press. Cherry Burton, 1987.

M. Fowler. Holderness Road, Through the Heart of East Hull, Highgate Publications (Beverley) Ltd. Beverley, 1990.

P. Gibson. Hull Pubs & Breweries, Tempus Publishing Ltd. Stroud, 2004.

P. Gibson. Hull Then & Now 4, paul-gibson.com. Hull, 2013.

P. Gibson. Images of Victorian Hull; F S Smith's Drawings of Hull Volume 3, paul-gibson.com. Hull, 2011.

P. Gibson. The Anlaby Road, Paul Gibson & The Friends of Lonsdale Community Centre. Hull, 2007.

P. Gibson and G. Wilkinson. Lost Pubs of Hull, Kingston Press. Hull, 1999.

I. N. Goldthorpe (edited by Margaret Sumner). Architecture of the Victorian Era of Kingston upon Hull; Being a Study of the Principal Buildings erected in Hull, 1830-1914, Highgate Publications (Beverley) Ltd. Beverley, 2005.

Ivan & Elixabeth Hall. A New Picture of Georgian Hull, William Sessions Ltd in association with Hull Civic Society. York, 1978.

M. Hindle. In Search of English Town Myton, Hull College Local History Unit. Hull, 1996.

C. Ketchell. Tremendous Activity in the Old Town; Demolitions Loss List 1943-1988, Hull College Local History Unit. Hull, 1989.

Kingston upon Hull City Transport. KHCT 1899-1979, Kingston upon Hull City Transport. Hull, 1979.

J. Markham. Streets of Hull: A History of their Names (2nd Ed.), Highgate Publications (Beverley) Ltd. Beverley, 1990.

R. Needler. Needler's of Hull, Hutton Press. Cherry Burton, 1993.

N. Pevsner and D. Neave. The Buildings of England; Yorkshire: York and the East Riding, Penguin Books, 1995.

B. N. Reckitt. The History of Reckitt & Sons Ltd, A Brown & Sons. Hull, 1952.

J. Richardson. History of the Streets of Hull, a Malet Lambert re-print of an original series of articles in the East Yorkshire Times in 1915. Hull, 1980s.

Sir A. K. Rollit and others. The City of Hull Official Handbook, with a Historical and Commercial Review. A. Brown & Sons. Hull, 1908.

John E. Smith. The Shop for the People, Two Centuries of Co-operative Enterprise in Hull and East Yorkshire, Hutton Press. Cherry Burton, 1998.

A. Wilkinson. From Corner Shop to Corner Shop in Five Generations, Hutton Press. Cherry Burton, 1994.

J. Wilson Smith. Inns of Holderness & Taverns of East Hull (Edited by Rob Barnard), Hull College Local History Unit. Hull, 1990s.

Other Sources:
Hull trade directories and telephone directories, various. Author's collection.
Ordnance Survey and other maps. Author's collection.
United Kingdom census returns. www.findmypast.co.uk
19th and 20th Century Newspapers. www.britishnewspaperarchive.co.uk
Modern satellite mapping and imagery. www.maps.google.co.uk
East Riding Museums short film. War Stories, Hull: Minesweeping; Anti-German Feeling.

Unpublished Sources:
P. Gibson. The Lost Pubs of Castle Street, Kingston Upon Hull. Hull, 2000.
P. Gibson. The Lost Hotels, Inns, Taverns & Beer-houses of Paragon Street. Hull, 2000.
P. Gibson. The Lost Public Houses of Prospect Street. Hull, 1999.
G. Wilkinson. Forgotten Hull. Notes to accompany the Health Department Collection of photographs. Hull, 2001.
G. Wilkinson. Landlord. Hull, 2007.

Thanks also, go to the following for their help: Rob Barnard, Alan Canvess, Susan Capes, Ian Halstead, Hull History Centre, Hull Museums (Wilberforce House), Steve Ingram, David Jessop, Bill Longbones, Mike Pearson, special thanks to David & Susan Neave, Caroline Rhodes, Kevin Rymer, Sam Allon (Contracts) Ltd, Martin Taylor, Gail Thornton, John Wyles, and anyone else who has assisted – if I've forgotten – I'm truly sorry!

Some of my other books

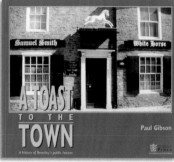

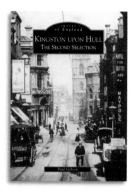

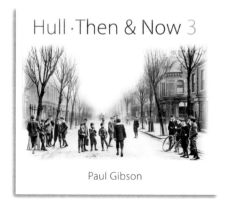

some other paul-gibson.com productions

Now Tigers!

The Early Years of Hull City
by Nicholas Turner

Hull City in the 1920s

Nicholas Turner

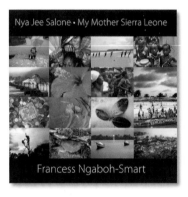

Nya Jee Salone • My Mother Sierra Leone

Francess Ngaboh-Smart

The Georgian Society for East Yorkshire
75th Anniversary

GEORGIAN ARCHITECTURE
&
THE GEORGIAN SOCIETY FOR
EAST YORKSHIRE
Austen Redman & David Neave

JAWBREAKER

POEMS BY
MIKE WATTS

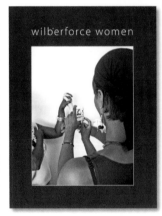

wilberforce women

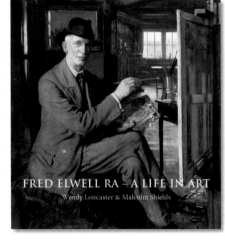

FRED ELWELL RA – A LIFE IN ART
Wendy Loncaster & Malcolm Shields